KALEIDOSCOPE

An Anthology

The Guild Writers

TGW

First Edition
December 2018

We express our appreciation to Marjorie Kopecek Nejdl
for her medallion in the style of Czech folk art
painted expressly for the cover of this book

ISBN: 9781728880945
Imprint: Independently published

KALEIDOSCOPE

Editing Team:
Carole Michalek Gauger
John Boswell Hudson
Sandra Cermak Hudson
Helga C. W. Mayhew
Mary Henkels Rhiner
Anneliese Heider Tisdale

Project Coordinator
Sandra Cermak Hudson

Book Design and Production
John Boswell Hudson
Sandra Cermak Hudson

Text is 11pt Century Schoolbook

Acknowledgements

We want to thank the
National Czech & Slovak Museum & Library
Cedar Rapids, Iowa for hosting us
and
The NCSML Guild for adopting us
as a special interest group

Authors are donating all proceeds
from the book sales to the
National Czech & Slovak Museum & Library

Author Sections

Kaleidoscope as metaphor:

The short memoirs and personal essays in this book are like the small gemstones in a kaleidoscope. They provide multiple perspectives as they tumble across your mind.

Introduction

Seventeen authors have contributed to this collection of short memoirs and personal essays. We invite you into our worlds. You'll find stories to fit most any mood—adventure, challenge, comedy, tragedy, quest, opportunity, success, failure, inspiration, and even self-discovery.

Kaleidoscope is designed to be read randomly. Jump in anywhere—a story here, another there. Flip a few pages in either direction, and you will find a new perspective. Just like looking into a kaleidoscope.

Some of our experiences may be similar to your own, some completely alien. Memoirs by definition are personal, yet in learning about us, we believe you will learn something of yourself. Should our stories awaken memories that linger in the recesses of your mind, we hope you will write them down. Everyone has stories to tell!

ENJOY THE MANY WORLDS
OF
KALEIDOSCOPE!

Anita Coufal Burke

Anita shares three excepts from her forthcoming book *The River Bottom Farm*. As a young child, Anita witnessed the tragedy of eminent domain. The government destroyed both her community and her family's livelihood when they took the family's five-hundred-acre farm to create the manmade Coralville Lake.

Until the age of ten Anita lived in Cou Falls, Iowa, a small unincorporated farming community which was settled in 1852 by her great-great-grandfather Josef Coufal and named for him, [aka, Cou Falls]. She remembers her Bohemian heritage, the twenty-one-room family home and the forty-two outbuildings that were demolished.

Anita's story is heartbreaking, yet she is thankful the Corps of Engineers saved the timber for a wildlife habitat, where she can still walk the paths and gather wild flowers. Those walks are bittersweet, as they are tangled with the pain of remembering the loss of that lovely one-hundred-year-old family farm.

River Bottom Farm

This picturesque twenty-one room farmhouse was built by three generations of Coufals: my great-great-grandfather, Josef; my great-grandfather, Joseph; and my grandfather, Joseph C. They built using trees harvested from their timber and milled in their sawmill.

The ground they cleared for the home was north of the Iowa River and south of what would become the small country village of Cou Falls. The name Cou Falls is an adaptation of my maiden name Coufal. Josef arrived in this country from Bohemia in 1850. He purchased thousands of acres of rich bottomland and then encouraged, and enabled, other Bohemian immigrants to join him. Together they built a community.

I have many fond memories of this gracious home with its L-shaped veranda and elaborate lattice. At one time, the lattice supported a vibrant wisteria vine, which twined its way upward. For me that lattice is a metaphor for how my great-great-grandfather supported his countrymen and helped them to thrive.

His grandson (my grandfather), Joseph C. Coufal, was skilled with a lathe, which was evident in the ornate trusses decorating the multiple gables of this home. Two additional architectural features were popular in the days before air conditioning: the screened porch was appreciated as a place to dine on hot summer days, and the screened second-floor sleeping porch captured the prairie breezes on sweltering summer nights.

Building that home, and the forty-two out buildings to create our farm was a labor of love for my ancestors. Yet today that farmstead is no more than a memory that lingers in my mind, and the mind of my oldest sister Elaine. It was all lost to eminent domain in the early 1950s. The United States Army Corps of Engineers removed or leveled every building on our farm, as well as those on neighboring farms, before damming the Iowa River to create the man-made Coralville Reservoir and Recreation Area.

I was ten when we lost the farm. Therefore, many of my stories are from the perspective of a ten-year-old. I have written about every aspect of my childhood sanctuary, though in this anthology I include only The Attic, and The Timber on the Hill. In my book, The River Bottom Farm, I share stories about other rooms in our farmhouse, the forty-two outbuildings that were my playground, the pond where we ice skated, the creek that sparkled with crystal clear water where my sister Darlene and I waded, and the Iowa River where I occasionally went with my father to catch fish to stock our pond.

Anita Coufal Burke

The Attic

So! Let's go up the stairs to the huge attic that I love to play in and do some snooping.

There are two flights of stairs. The first flight is carpeted and leads to a long hallway with four bedrooms, a linen room, and a bathroom. At the end of the hallway and around a corner is the door to the attic. I open the door and we see a flight of wooden steps. There is a light switch on the wall, but I don't turn it on because so much light comes in through the large attic windows.

The attic itself is a large open area with planed oak floors, and three large floor-length windows with lace curtains. There is a wooden fenced area at the head of the stairs to keep wrapping papers, holiday things, and toilet paper, which we buy in large quantities because of our big family and hired help. I often wonder why this area is fenced in. Could it have had another use at one time?

Everything in this attic has a place and is well organized. There are many old wooden trunks that came over with my ancestors when they arrived from Bohemia. Some are full of Babi (Grandmother) Coufal's clothes, which are black or blue fancy dresses. Babi died of a stroke when she was only fifty-four. My mom talks about her a lot and how she was such a sweet, loving person.

My dad's sister, Aunt Mildred, stored dressers, tables, and many boxes when she moved to California. There have been many old keepsakes stored in the attic over the years by the previous three generations of Coufals that have lived in this home.

Darlene and I get into everything in the attic as no one checks on us. Mom is too busy tending to all her chores and household duties. We try playing Dad's old push-button accordion, and the big trombone. We secretly play dress up with Babi's old clothes. My aunts would have a fit if they knew this.

We store some of our playthings and doll clothes in the old dressers. The attic is not a cluttered area. Unlike a lot of attics, ours is so neat and clean. We carefully put everything away just as we found it when we are done playing.

In the winter, the heat from the chimney keeps the attic slightly warm. Mom carries baskets of clothes from the basement up three flights of stairs. My oldest sister, Elaine, has to help. They hang the clothes all over the attic to dry. Those that aren't near the chimney freeze. Freeze solid! The coveralls can even stand up on the floor all by themselves.

My sister, Darlene, and I play up here a lot. Come see my dolls and doll furniture. This bassinet is special. Sometimes I carry little buckets of water from the second-floor bathroom to pour it into my bassinet to give my dolls their baths. This hose at the bottom has a clamp that I can open to drain the water. I'm always careful not to spill a drop. Then I carry the water back down to the bathroom.

This is my beauty shop. It's really a doll high chair. It's where I cut my doll's hair. Then I style it with these little pink hair rollers. I also polish their fingernails and toenails.

One time I found a very old doll that belonged to my oldest sister, Elaine. I decided to beautify her. So I painted her nails and cut her hair to give her a new look. Elaine was devastated. She cherished that doll. I felt bad. I didn't mean to ruin her keepsake. Oh, yes, I did get in trouble for that.

Last Christmas, Mom said I was too old for a doll, but I really wanted one. Elaine, being my mother hen that she always is, told Mom she was going to buy one for me.

When Christmas came, sure enough, she gave me a doll with dark shoulder-length hair, and a blue dress, but she's the right size to wear some of my other doll's clothes also. She really looks like a "Patsy" to me. So that's what I call her. Patsy doesn't have bendable legs and arms like my other dolls, but I still bring her up here for baths anyway. Patsy never visits my beauty shop.

Elaine doesn't live here anymore. She graduated from Iowa City High and works in Cedar Rapids. Sometimes though, she comes home for weekends. I really miss her. She and I had always shared the same bedroom, and even slept together. Now she's gone. Sometimes it makes me mad. Sometimes sad. It helps to have my Little Elaine. She's a special doll that I've named after my big sister.

I take Little Elaine with me everywhere. Isn't she cute? So soft and cuddly. I like her pink outfit with the hooded green jacket. The colors are light, they remind me of the mints Mom puts out when people come over to play cards.

Look at this. The fingers on her right hand are curled except her thumb, which sticks up so she can suck it, with my help! And her left hand is open, so I can help her to wave "hi" or "good-bye". Aren't her nails beautiful? I painted them in my beauty shop.

Little Elaine has three different faces, but you can only see one face at a time. That's 'cause her bonnet hides the other two faces. This knob in the shape of a bow on top of her head is sticking up through her bonnet. When I turn it, her head goes around. You can see Little Elaine's baby face smile, or cry, or sleep.

Kaleidoscope

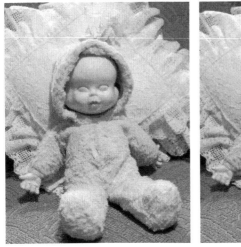 

Little Elaine

When I put Little Elaine down for a nap, I always show her sleeping face. Sometimes though, when I go back to get her, my teenage brother, Merle, has rotated her head to make her cry. He does that a lot. It makes me very mad! He loves to tease me, even though we're best buddies.

My Little Elaine has been through a lot. The worst was the day when Dad and the hired men came in after a long day in the fields. They settled themselves on upside-down five-gallon buckets in the front yard just off the front porch. They were having a good time talking and drinking beer.

I wanted to show off Little Elaine. One of the hired men. gave her a drink of his beer; spilling it all over her. I ran into the house crying. The tears were streaming down my face.

Mom washed Little Elaine, but she was never the same after her drink of beer. Now, when I push the spring squeaker in her tummy, she doesn't make a sound. Her squeaker is broken, and so is my heart.

* * * * *

It is now sixty years since I had to say "goodbye" to this farm. Little Elaine has seen me cry a lot. Mom and Dad had never told me we were going to move far away from here until the time it was about to happen. I missed my aunts and uncles, Deda and Mary (my step-grandmother), and my friends. I developed a hate for the Corps of Engineers when I heard what was going to happen to our farm, the only playground I had ever known. However, Little Elaine has been there with me through all my many moves, even now that I'm grown and married. She will always have a special place in my heart.

Timber on the Hill

When the Corps of Engineers took our five-hundred-acre farm south of the village of Cou Falls to create the Coralville Reservoir, they told my dad he could keep the timber. His reply was, "I'm a farmer! What good is this timber on a hill going to do for me?" He was informed that if he decided not to keep it, the timber would be part of the eminent domain acquisition and would become a wildlife preserve.

When this started happening, I was around five years old. After all these years, I have discovered our timber has never been kept on their books as a preserve. The land is considered a wildlife habitat, and therefore, hunting is permitted. I guess I really don't mind, since I still visit this timber that I so dearly loved as a child.

Back then, the timber was always clean, without underbrush, just as timberland had been maintained in Bohemia where my great-great-grandfather grew up. Dad would allow our cattle to graze in this timber since it went down to our creek on the north side. From the top of the hill to the road was pasture.

Trees from this timber were used to construct all of the buildings on two farmsteads, as far back as my great-great-grandparents. The tree branches and what was left over after the lumber was cut and milled in our family sawmill, was used to heat the houses, workshop, and other buildings.

There were supposed to be Indian mounds in the timber. My sister Darlene and I would get a shovel and begin to dig in what we believed to be an Indian mound. Then we'd get scared that a ghost would come out and run for home. Deda (Grandfather) Coufal told us of finding Indian arrowheads when the new road was built.

Deda's house

Darlene and I used the old road to visit Deda. The new road was too busy, and Mom didn't want us on it. We would pull our wagons along the old road, then through the timber and down the steep hill behind Deda's house to get watermelons and muskmelons. After Deda had filled our wagons with the melons, we would head back up that steep hill, pulling and tugging our heavy load, but not before enjoying fresh-made cookies from Deda's pantry.

And oh, so many wild flowers grew in the timber: Dutchman britches, bluebells, jack-in-the-pulpits, sweet Williams, violets, and columbine. On May Day, we picked wild flowers to fill our May baskets. First, we would color cone-shaped paper cups, the kind that we used for drinking water at our one-room schoolhouse. Then, we'd use one of Dad's pipe cleaners to add a handle, before adding a little water, and the wildflowers. To surprise Babi (Grandmother) and Deda, we would hang the basket on their door knob, ring the door bell, and run away. This was the tradition before it became popular to put candy in May baskets.

The timber was also full of all kinds of nut trees—walnut, hickory nut, butternut, and hazelnut. Mom would make her famous hickory nut cake that everyone loved. However, it was we kids who had to clean the hickory nuts. It was quite a task. They're not the easiest nut to shell without getting shells in with the nutmeats.

Dad also did his mushroom hunting in this timber, and would always know where to go. He took us along sometimes. We'd walk right over the mushrooms and not see them; however, Dad did and would pick them. In my mind's eye, I can see him now—that green visor cap he always wore, the denim coveralls, and his pocket knife ready in one hand, and a paper sack in the other hand.

In the fall the timber was picturesque against blue sky with fluffy white clouds. It was like opening a box of crayons with the yellow, red, orange, and brown leaves getting ready for winter.

It has now been over sixty years since I played in this timber. To most people it may be just timber. They may drive the dusty road and not see all the beauty I see. Or understand why I am drawn back to this river bottom.

It is so sad to see how the timber looks now. It is no longer clean, there is underbrush, fallen trees, and layers and layers of leaves. As I walk the path that had been the old road, I can't believe all the empty bottles and cans people have left behind. There is even a pile of Christmas cards someone had dumped on the path—I can still read the insides of the cards. There are ruts from four-wheelers all over, and the DNR has carved out some of the hill for a building to house their equipment. Most of the song birds aren't there anymore.

I can't help but have tears running down my cheeks as I walk past one of Dad's fence posts with the wire still attached. My eyes are searching for the flowers I remember—Dutchmen britches covering the timber hillside like a sea of white each spring, and then bluebells appearing with their blue and pink colors, and jack-in-the-pulpits that I so loved.

I follow the pathway that used to be the old road. Going off the path to a sunny spot toward the creek, there they are! With excitement, I yell for my husband, "Bill, I've found some bluebells!" The flowers are just popping up.

Okay, I know I'm in the right place now, so I walk further down the hill toward the creek and pretty soon I see the Dutchmen britches growing amidst the underbrush and many roots.

I head the other direction toward the road and the hilltop where I find some columbine. Bill yells to me to come toward the big trees further up the hill. There we see bluebells and Dutchmen britches everywhere. We continue to find more and more. I'm as excited as a little kid.

After we return home, I tell my daughter Kim and granddaughter Maci what we discovered. They also want to see the timber of my childhood. So, a few days later Bill, Kim, Maci, and I head down to the timber. The woods are full of even more flowers. Maci wanders off and yells to us, "I found a big patch of bluebells!" Indeed she has.

Granddaughter Maci

We walk the old road to Deda's house just as I had done decades ago with my little red wagon. As we get closer to the top of the hill, we see them to the side of the path—the whole hillside is a sea of white with Dutchmen britches just like I remember. What a lovely sight. Memories flood my mind. Should I be glad that the government took our farm from us to build Coralville Reservoir? Would the timber still be here for me and others to enjoy if it had not been preserved as a wildlife habitat?

We keep walking the path to Deda's house which seems much further than when I was younger. At the top of the hill we look toward the Iowa River and the green hillside that slopes down to Deda's house, which is still standing. It is such a lovely view, even though the whole bottomland is covered with waterways and silt left behind from floods. The channel of the Iowa River is way-off in the distance, but I recognize it. It has not changed. All of this land, as far as we can see, had been our family farm before it was flooded by the Corps of Engineers to make the Coralville Reservoir.

On the way back to our vehicles I show them the fence post and part of the wire fence Dad had put there to keep our cattle from venturing over to Deda's. I can't believe those remnants are still there.

Mayapples are growing all over. I tell my family how Darlene and I would take them and hit them against a tree to make a schussing sound.

We keep finding more and more flowers. I almost step on a jack-in-the-pulpit, then two more. Exhausted after a wonderful day, we head back to our cars. As we walk back through the gate and fence toward where the big chicken house once stood, we look back at this lovely timber.

Our day in the timber with Kim and Maci is complete. This is something they will now be able to associate with my many stories. Each time they see it they will remember all the joy that this timber still brings to me.

Maci   Kim   Anita

Racheal Gangestad Davis

Racheal has loved stories from the moment she understood them. She is the keeper, teller, and recorder of family stories, the archivist of family history and documents,
and the curator of heirlooms.

Wife, daughter, patriot, friend, teacher, librarian,
mentor, caregiver, reader, collector, lifelong Iowan, and
world traveler all describe Racheal.

Racheal has a deep interest in classical music, history, travel, genealogy, art, architecture, and literature.

Her memoir writing evolves from her heritage and
many unique life experiences. She finds value, beauty,
humor, and inspiration in the great and commonplace.

The Midnight Ride

Listen, one and all, and you shall hear of the famous midnight ride of someone other than Paul Revere.

The person of whom I speak is Major William Dawes, Jr., my great-great-great-great grandfather. The ride, made famous by Longfellow's poem, took place April 18, 1775. Its purpose was to send out the alarm to every village and farm for the Minutemen to assemble, to warn Samuel Adams and John Hancock that the British were coming to Lexington intent on arresting them, and to ensure the concealment of arms and ammunition at Concord because the British planned to confiscate them.

William Dawes has been called the first rider for the revolution because Dr. Joseph Warren, a leader of the Committee on Correspondence, sent for Dawes first. Dawes began his ride out of Boston one hour before the other rider.

William Dawes, the fifth generation of our family to reside in North America, was part of a large group of colonists who resisted the oppressive rule of the British. He was a Minute Man, Son of Liberty, Major in the Ancient and Honorable Artillery Company of Massachusetts, and a member of Old South Church. As part of this group of patriots, he conspired against the British, met secretly in smoke-filled attics, served as a courier and spy, and danced around the Liberty Tree. He was also in a group of thirty spies known as "mechanics," who patrolled the streets of Boston day and night attempting to watch every move made by the British.

As a result of intelligence thus collected, Dr. Joseph Warren sent a message to William Dawes at 65 Ann Street in Boston just before ten o'clock on the evening of April 18, 1775. Thirty-year-old William kissed his pretty little wife Mehitable, told her nothing, left his home, and walked the short distance to Dr. Warren's home.

After receiving very detailed orders, Dawes walked to the stable behind his tannery on Friend Street, saddled his horse, and rode quietly through back streets. He passed through the British sentinel on Boston Neck by mixing in with some Redcoats in the darkness. His uncle Josiah Waters had followed on foot to watch his progress. After seeing his nephew pass the sentinel on Boston Neck, he reported this to Dr. Warren.

William Dawes galloped to Roxbury where he relayed Dr. Warren's orders to General Heath. He continued through Brookline, all the while alerting residents along the way. He crossed the Charles River on the Great Bridge and entered Cambridge. He warned the militia that the Redcoats were coming and relayed Dr. Warren's order to deplank the Great Bridge. The militia and some Harvard students sprang to the task. At Menotomy he gave messages to the Committee of Safety.

Onward he galloped to Lexington where he went to the Hancock-Clark house to warn Samuel Adams and John Hancock that the British were coming to arrest them. They immediately went into hiding and eluded capture.

Dawes and the other rider dispatched by Dr. Warren met at the Hancock-Clark house. About 12:30 in the morning of April 19th, they departed for the six-mile journey to Concord. On the road, they met Dr. Samuel Prescott, who had been out late courting his sweetheart. When they were satisfied that he was a "high son of liberty" they allowed him to ride with them.

At times they encountered Redcoats on patrol. At one o'clock in the morning the other rider, Paul Revere, was captured and held by the British. Therefore, he did not complete his ride to Concord. Dr. Prescott eluded capture by jumping his horse over a stone wall. William Dawes led the Redcoats pursuing him up to a farmhouse shouting, "I've got two of them." Suspecting an ambush, the Redcoats hastily rode away. Dawes had stopped his horse so abruptly that he was thrown off. He returned a few days later to retrieve his pocket watch from the spot where he landed.

"William Who Rode" continued to Concord alone. Upon arriving there he assisted in hiding two small cannons nicknamed "Hancock" and "Adams."

The Minutemen were coming from all directions to assemble near the North Bridge. Among them was Jonas Holden, another of my great-great-great-great grandfathers.

When the British arrived, they and the Minutemen faced one another across the North Bridge. Without any orders being given, a shot rang out. It is unknown from which side it came. It has been called "the shot heard round the world." The war for American independence had begun.

The descendants of "William Who Rode" have commemorated the patriotism of their heroic ancestor in various ways. For many years I sent handmade greeting cards to other descendants on the anniversary of the ride. Poems have been written, books published, ceremonies held, memorials erected. The ride is commemorated as Patriots' Day in Massachusetts, and the Daughters of the American Revolution honor the ride by beginning its Continental Congress on the Monday of the week containing April 18.

In 1971, one hundred ninety-six years after the ride, my cousin George E. Dawes, my mother Ruth Dawes Gangestad, and I, Racheal Gangestad Davis, founded the Descendants of William Who Rode Association and became its charter officers. Forty-seven years later it is an international organization with more than two hundred proud, enthusiastic, active members from the United States, Canada, and Australia.

We decided to call the first rider for the American Revolution "William Who Rode" to distinguish him from all the other William Dawes above him and below him in the Dawes family tree, which we trace to 1492 in England.

Racheal Gangestad Davis

The Baptism

After fifteen years of marriage and adopting two children, my sister and her husband were amazed to be told that they were expecting a baby.

My thirty-seven-year-old sister sought out a highly recommended obstetrician. This Jewish doctor had privileges at Barnes Jewish Hospital in St. Louis. My nephew was born there May 23, 1970. Although he was a full-term baby, he had not gained any weight during the ninth month of pregnancy. So this low-weight, fragile baby was placed in an incubator.

The doctor advised the parents that if there were a religious ritual they wanted performed, it should be done immediately. A phone call was quickly made to their Lutheran pastor, Dr. Walker. He came to the hospital as fast as he could. The pastor was capped, gowned, and gloved by a nurse and taken into the nursery.

As the parents watched, the nurse asked, "What do you Lutherans use for baptism?"

"Water," Dr. Walker replied.

"Did you bring some with you?"

"No."

Trying to be helpful the nurse said, "A Catholic priest was here a couple of months ago. He brought holy water. We put it in a medicine bottle that has an eye dropper. There is some left. Do you want to use that?"

"Yes, certainly."

So, it came to pass that my nephew Philip, son of Rebecca and Loren Ahlrichs, was baptized in a Jewish hospital, by a Lutheran clergyman, using Catholic holy water.

What an ecumenical baby! The most ecumenical baby that I have ever known.

The Tulips

My friend, classmate, and next-door neighbor, Carol Tollefsrud, and I walked to and from school together.

In the spring of the year that Carol and I were in first grade, we became very enchanted with a bed of tulips that we passed four times a day, five days a week. We passed it on our way to school in the morning. We passed it at noon walking home for lunch. We passed it going back for afternoon classes. Then, at the end of the school day, we passed it going home. This was when we could linger.

In fascination we watched the progress of the tulip plants from the first bit of green that poked through the black soil to the point where a small bud topped the tulip stem. We watched the buds grow larger. Then, the buds expanded enough that seams gaped, and we could detect the color. What a welcome sight the blooms would be after a long hard winter such as we had back in those times in northwest Iowa.

Then, a glorious day arrived when Carol and I stood on the sidewalk gazing at red and yellow tulips. They were beautiful. We held our breath in awe. We stood motionless, transfixed. We wanted to touch the beautiful flowers. It would be even better to hold them in our hands. And, wouldn't it be even more wonderful to show them to our mothers? Oh yes, it surely would be.

But, Carol and I did not reach forth a hand. Our whole lives we had been taught that it is a sin to steal. We knew we must leave the tulips just where they were. So we did leave them, slowly, unhappily.

We walked south another block and a half before turning east. Immediately, we saw tulips in bloom up by the foundation of the first house. We gasped with pleasure. Another opportunity.

Then both Carol and I held several tulips in our hands. We ran diagonally across the street. We parted in my back yard. Carol headed for the back door of the parsonage, and I headed for my back door. Anticipating a joyous reception, we hurried forth with bouquets for our mothers.

I don't know what happened in the parsonage, but my mother was far from pleased. When Daddy came home, he and Mother discussed the matter. Then I was informed that I must go back to the house where the tulips had lived, knock on the door, and tell whomever answered the door that I had stolen some of their tulips, that I was very sorry, and that I would never ever do such a thing again.

My heart must have fallen into my shoes, for that was where Superintendent of Schools E. O. Berkland lived. I was terrified of Superintendent E. O. Berkland. He was always so stern. But do it I must.

Daddy walked with me holding my hand. We crossed the street. Daddy stopped in their driveway and sent me to cross their backyard alone, go up the steps, and knock on the kitchen door.

When Superintendent E. O. Berkland answered the door, he looked down at me sternly. I was very nervous and scared. My throat was dry. With some effort I found my voice and softly said, "I just thought I should come over here and tell you that Carol Tollefsrud picked some of your tulips."

A Night to Remember

On a cold, moonlight, December night during the Second World War, Mother, Daddy, Becky, my aunt, my cousin, and I crowded into Daddy's1938, blue, two-door Ford V8. Our destination, some twenty miles from Bode, was the prisoner of war camp just west of Algona, Iowa, where we were to view a nativity scene created by six German prisoners of war. During the war we had not often driven out of town because of the rationing of gasoline and rubber. Doing so now set this evening apart from others.

Upon our arrival we were struck by the height of the fence surrounding the camp. What a strange thing it was to see Daddy speaking to the man with a gun, who stopped us at the gate. How surprising that this man shone his big flashlight on each of us in both the front and back seats. Then he inspected the car's trunk. Instructions followed at Daddy's window. Daddy drove forward. We were inside the tall fence now. It was amazing to realize we were inside a prison.

Then we were in a cold, dimly-lit barrack sitting on plank and tile benches looking at the nativity scene and Christmas tree at the far end of the room. There were sixty-five half-life-size figures in the nativity scene which seemed to fill the narrow end of the barrack. The prisoners who had built it purchased materials with money they earned working on nearby farms.

In the distance we heard the cadence of marching feet on frozen ground. The sound grew louder, closer. Doors opened abruptly. Armed guards escorted a group of prisoners into the front of the room. The prisoners formed two rows in front of the Christmas tree and faced us. They began to sing a cappella. Their voices were beautiful.

Although we didn't know the German language, we soon realized that we knew the songs they were singing, because we knew the melodies. They were singing our Christmas carols.

What a lot for us children to ponder as we rode home in the moonlight gazing at the bare trees raising their arms to heaven and casting beautiful shadows on snow-covered fields. Now we knew that our enemy knew the same Christmas carols we did. Did this mean that they knew the same god? Then, why were we killing one another?

And on that night only God knew that some fifty years on, Racheal, the little American girl from Bode, Iowa, and Kurt Butzlaff, one of the German prisoners of war who sang that night, would meet with conciliatory hearts, not at far ends of a long room, but close enough to touch and hug tightly, marveling in the discovery that they had shared that extraordinary evening decades earlier in a prison camp in the midst of a long, horrible, costly war.

Racheal Davis and Kurt Butzlaff

The Dawes Girls

Puzzle Solved

My maternal grandfather Richmond Meade Dawes was known to everyone as Rich. And he was known by a lot of people in Buchanan County, Iowa. Mother told me that when she walked down the street in Independence with her father; everyone seemed to know him and greet him.

"Hello, Rich."

"Hey, Rich."

"Good morning, Rich."

Rich met a young lady, Evelena Georgiana Wise, in the mid-1890s when they were attending Iowa State Normal School in Cedar Falls. When they completed their studies, each of them taught in a one-room country school near the small town of Winthrop and their respective family farms.

Rich's teaching career came to an abrupt halt on April 25, 1898, when President William McKinley declared war on Spain. Word of this came to Iowa by telegraph.

Early the next morning Rich drove his brother's team and wagon to the school and wrote, "Gone to War. R. M. Dawes" on the blackboard. He left the team and wagon in the schoolyard, walked into Winthrop, boarded a train, and was off to join the army.

Evelena continued teaching while Rich was "gone to war." However, when Rich came home from the Spanish-American War and they were married in August 1900, Evelena's teaching career was over. In those days it was thought that the teaching positions should be given to single women who had to support themselves. Married women were supported by their husbands.

Rich and Evelena had four daughters, Vera, Verna, Ruth, and Florence, who came to be known as the Dawes girls. And they never stopped thinking of themselves as the girls.

All of the Dawes girls went to Iowa State Teachers College in Cedar Falls and became teachers. In the next generation, two of us became teachers. The tradition lived on.

All of us had very interesting and remarkable experiences in our teaching careers. So, we had many stories to share, such as the one following.

When Aunt Florence was teaching in Ida Grove, Iowa, in the mid-1930s, it became known around school that her folks were going to California to spend the winter. The other teachers were truly amazed. How, they wondered, could anyone afford that? It was the Great Depression, after all. Some of them came from families that were struggling to survive and hang onto the mortgaged farm.

Then the faculty learned that Aunt Florence was also going to California to spend Christmas. And, in addition to the two-week school vacation, she was taking two more weeks without pay. She would be gone one month.

The others were absolutely dumbfounded. How could she afford a round-trip train fare? More to the point, how could she possibly forego two weeks salary? None of them had the money to do such a thing. Curiosity grew and grew. There were sidelong glances, probing questions, speculation behind her back, and some ill-concealed envy on their faces.

Aunt Florence felt no need to justify her plans or to explain her finances. So, she didn't.

December came. Aunt Florence went. January came. Aunt Florence returned. Although she had been gone a month, she found the other teachers were still mystified, envious, and wildly curious.

Then something happened that cleared everything up for them. The state teachers convention in Des Moines rolled around. The Ida Grove teachers boarded the train for Des Moines.

There were enough empty seats that they were able to sit together. At one of the stops a lady boarded. As she came down the aisle, her facial expression changed to recognition, surprise, and pleasure.

She stopped in front of Aunt Florence and said, "Aren't you one of the Rich Dawes girls?" The eyes of the other teachers grew big. They leaned in. They inhaled through open slack-jawed mouths.

"Yes," Aunt Florence said, "I am."

The Apples

One fall Aunt Vera was hired to substitute teach in the same first grade classroom for two weeks. The first day, after returning from lunch at home, a little boy named Bobby presented Aunt Vera with an apple. She thanked him warmly and gave him a big smile. He seemed very pleased with himself. Perhaps he looked a bit taller as he walked to his desk.

The next day the scene repeated itself. And on the next day, and on the next day. Liking the thanks and attention, he brought Aunt Vera an apple every day for two weeks. Each afternoon she carried the apple home and put it in a cool place.

Now Aunt Vera knew her apple varieties, and she had noticed that each day's apple was a different variety—Wealthy, Jonathan, Winesap, Grimes Golden, Northern Spy, and so on. So, when Bobby presented the tenth apple, yet another variety, on her last day of substituting, she said to him, "My goodness, your parents must really have quite an orchard to have so many kinds of apples."

"No," he said, "we don't have any apple trees at all. I just went into a different yard every time."

Ten apples. Ten varieties.

The following Sunday Aunt Vera rose early, baked an apple pie, put a beef roast in the oven, and went to church. She had volunteered to entertain the visiting bishop and his wife for dinner. When she served the meal, the bishop, his preaching duties over for the day, really seemed to be relishing it. Then when Aunt Vera served the apple pie with the wonderful flaky crust, his enjoyment increased many-fold. He savored each bite.

"Oh my, this is very, very good," he said. "Delicious," he added. "Mrs. Giermann, just what kind of apples did you put in this pie?"

"Stolen," Aunt Vera replied.

"I beg your pardon?"

"Stolen."

One Day at Wrigley Field

It is a beautiful day in Chicago. It is June 1948. Aunt Florence is taking my older sister Becky, my mother Ruth, and me to our first major league baseball game at Wrigley Field. The Brooklyn Dodgers are in town to play the Cubs.

Our seats are above third base. Becky and I sit in one row. Mother and Aunt Florence sit directly behind us.

My fifteen-year-old sister Becky is the most knowledgeable and the most informed of us all concerning baseball. She reads the sports page every day, she listens to sports news and games on the radio, and she and Daddy talk about baseball.

The Cubs are up at bat, and the Dodgers take the field. Becky sees the third baseman, recognizes him, and becomes very, very excited. Pointing unobtrusively down to third base, she pokes me and says, "There's Jackie Robinson!"

I look. I see a big broad-shouldered guy in a Dodger's uniform. I nod. I see no need to reveal to my big sister that I have no idea who Jackie Robinson is or why she is so excited.

Becky turns toward Mother and Aunt Florence. "There's Jackie Robinson," she proclaims joyfully. Mother and Aunt Florence look to where she is pointing, but say nothing. Becky turns to them again, repeats herself, tries to elicit the response this momentous occasion deserves. They nod and look again. They have no idea who Jackie Robinson is or why his presence is important.

A Cub is up at bat. Becky turns her attention to that. She is ready to mark her scorecard. Behind me, I hear Aunt Florence's voice say, "Why, Ruth, I do believe he's colored."

Many decades later I meet Art Pennington, a friend of my husband. Art played in the Negro League with Jackie. I tell him that I saw Jackie play way back in his second season in the majors. Art says that there were many in the Negro League who were better players than Jackie Robinson, but Branch Rickey chose Jackie for his temperament, patience, and the self-control that would be required of the one who broke the color barrier in baseball.

Staying at the Paris Grand

One July day Mother, Daddy, Aunt Florence, and I woke in our hotel near the fashionable walking street in Copenhagen. Aunt Florence, an early riser, went out for Danish pastries, which we enjoyed with coffee before checking out of our rooms. It was a beautiful, sunny day, and though we were reluctant to leave Denmark, which we had found so delightful, we enjoyed our ride to the airport. There we boarded a plane for Paris. After a short, smooth flight we landed at Orly Field.

We rode into Paris and arrived at the Grand Hotel where we had reservations for two rooms. At the hotel desk the concierge found our reservations, asked for our passports, and copied the numbers. Our day had been flowing along swimmingly. We were in Paris.

The Louvre was beckoning to us, and it was not yet 11am. Then the concierge informed us that our rooms were not ready. Disappointment and dismay appeared on our faces. The concierge offered us seating in a private alcove of the beautiful lobby. We declined. He suggested that we stroll across the street to the Opera House. We declined. The dining room would accommodate us for an early lunch. We declined. Negotiations continued. After a while the concierge acknowledged that one of our rooms was now ready. He proposed that all of us and all of our luggage be taken to that room, and later the staff would move two of us to the second room. We accepted.

Once we were ensconced in the room, Daddy decided that he wanted to stay there for a nap. The rest of us prepared to depart for the Louvre. Then Daddy sat up in bed and said he needed the room key in case he woke before we returned and wanted to go for a stroll. We needed a key in case Daddy wasn't there when we returned. Aunt

Florence phoned the desk and asked that a second key be brought to us. The person on the other end of the line was not the concierge we had dealt with earlier. This voice neither spoke nor understood English very well. When he was asked to send a key up to us, he perplexedly said, "You have key."

Yes, we had one key, but we needed two. Aunt Florence tried without success to explain the need for two keys. Eventually, the exchange reached the point where Aunt Florence asked over and over, "Is there more than one key to this room?" Finally, finally, finally it seemed that there was. "Bring us that key tout suite," she said.

After a fretful and seemingly long wait, we heard a knock. So anxious were we that three of us converged on the door in a flash. We yanked it open. There stood a uniformed man holding a tray bearing a tea pot, a cream pitcher, a hot water pitcher, a sugar bowl, two cups, two saucers, two spoons, and two linen napkins.

"Where is the key?"

He offered the tea tray. We waved it away.

"The key! Not tea, key!"

He looked bewildered. The one key we possessed was held up.

"Key, key, key," each of us said impatiently. In a slow deliberate voice pronouncing each word distinctly, Aunt Florence said, "Go get the key and bring it quickly." She pointed to the lock on our door, displayed the key we had, and held up two fingers. Through all of this the man's face remained uncomprehending. He did seem to understand he was being sent away, and he stepped backward ever so slightly.

"Tout suite," Aunt Florence asserted, and waved him away.

The man pivoted, stopped in mid-pivot, turned back and asked, "You want tea?"

Racheal Gangestad Davis

Sunday Dinner with a P.K.

I married a P.K. Besides the joy of loving him dearly and basking in his love and devotion, it was quite an adventure. Early on I became aware that Seth was not as awed by authority figures as I. Nor did he observe as many unwritten rules as I did.

For example, one Sunday he wore a new pair of shoes to church. As we walked from the parking lot, he complained about the shoes pinching his feet. Too late to do anything about it now, I thought. He would just have to endure. After the service had begun Seth leaned down to untie his shoes. Afraid of what was to follow, I leaned over and hissed, "You can't take your shoes off in church."

"Yes, I can," he replied and did so. I was aghast. Thank goodness, he was wearing new socks, no holes. I considered pretending that I was not with him and had no idea who he was. I had to abandon that notion because we had been seen holding hands, and we were sitting so close together that a miser's offering-envelope could not have been slipped between our shoulders.

Seth was not the first or only P.K. I had known. There were some in my hometown over the years and, of course, we knew them. One of them even lived with us when her parents were sent overseas.

When I arrived at Wartburg College I was surrounded by P.K.s. The place was crawling with them. In that environment I even found myself on the path to potentially becoming the mother of P.K.s. The romance waned and I was liberated from such a future.

Some years later, I did become an aunt by marriage to four P.K.s. I do not often volunteer that information, as two of them as kids, playing with matches, caused a fire that destroyed a one-hundred-year-old building at the historic Washington Prairie Lutheran Church campus south of Decorah.

Upon college graduation I left the P.K.s, the pre-thes, the Christian day-school majors, the choir clique, the pre-meds, the jocks, the cheerleaders, the North Hall boys, the radio station gang, the Little Theater group, and all the rest at Wartburg behind me to begin my teaching career in Mason City, Iowa.

One Saturday afternoon while living there I entered a small shop downtown to buy a typewriter ribbon. As I left the shop, I was laughing over a comment made by the shopkeeper. I opened the door and stepped directly into the path of a P.K. from Wartburg! He thought the big smile was meant for him. Both of us stopped before colliding.

Within days we had our first date. Within two months we were engaged. Of course, I took him home to meet my parents as soon as our relationship became serious—in other words, almost right away.

My family always attended church at 10:30 Sunday morning. At noon we sat down to a formal dinner during which church was critiqued. Had the pastor adequately explained that day's scripture? Did we agree with his interpretation? Was the sermon more boring or less boring than usual? Had he said anything we didn't believe? Was the sermon too long? Why had he chosen unfamiliar hymns? Then there was the pastor's sarcasm that came with the announcements. Imagine him gruffly telling us that there was no need for anyone to knock over the Christmas trees in the chancel during the processional offering. When we had finished with him, at least for the moment, we moved on to his family. Why in the world hadn't his wife mended the torn and sagging hem in the center back of his surplice yet? From there we commented on the choir, organist, ushers, and parishioners.

However, when Seth, a P.K., was present at our Sunday dinner table, we were on our best behavior. Not one word, good or bad, was spoken about church.

As the months rolled by, my parents became so accustomed to Seth being with us, that one Sunday Daddy started saying something about the minister. He caught himself midway and stopped. Trying to recover he turned to Seth and said with a smile, "I don't suppose that in the parsonage you knew, the parishioners were having roast preacher for Sunday dinner."

Without a pause, Seth, who as a Preacher's Kid had grown up in parsonages, said with a smile, "We were having roast congregation."

Daddy (Leon), Mother (Ruth), Racheal, and her P.K. Seth

A Memorable Day

A soft gentle breeze off the English Channel brushes my face, swirls around me as I stand in an extraordinarily beautiful, otherworldly place. The sky is a magnificent blue. The grass is a most gorgeous green. White marble glistens brilliantly in the bright sun. I am transported to a reflective, restful place. I am deeply moved by the serenity, the ambience, the holy purpose of this place—the Normandy American Cemetery and Memorial on the cliff above Normandy Beach, France.

Twice I have had the privilege of visiting this special place. Today, my second visit, is especially memorable because it is Memorial Day at home. It is Memorial Day here, too. This is part of my home. As an American, as a free person, I am at home in this reverent, revered place. It is beautiful. The flags flutter at half-mast. An American flag graces every grave. My eyes travel over the countless rows of crosses and stars of David. Name after name engraved in white marble. Name after name after name. How surprising it is that the strongest emotion I feel is peacefulness. All are at rest here.

God is here. His presence enfolds the quick and the dead. His soft breeze touches every blade of the grassy blanket covering every fallen hero. His radiant sun gleams on every marble marker.

I think of Paul, the eldest son of my parents' dear friends. As a little girl I so admired this handsome big boy with the wonderful smile. He was a pilot shot down during the Battle of the Bulge.

I think of my cousin John Thorson Jr., who threw himself on an enemy grenade to save his comrades and was awarded the Medal of Honor posthumously.

There are so many heroes. Some are noted for an outstanding feat. Others contributed in many, many ways, among them dutifully and bravely keeping on keeping on.

How thought-provoking it is that these fallen in the evil, hatred, ugliness, and violence of war, rest in such a peaceful, serene place of beauty. What a humbling privilege it is for me to be in this resting place of the fallen, to pay my respect and gratitude, and to cherish the freedom for which they fought and died.

Normandy American Cemetery and Memorial
Photo from the American Battle Monuments Commission

Carole Michalek Gauger

Horses and horsepower are Carole's life-long passion. As a horsewoman, she is a two-time national champion, and a four-term president of the renowned *U.S. Lipizzan Registry*. She has traveled to Austria to study pedigrees, breeding practices, and riding techniques with the celebrated Chief Rider of the Spanish Riding School. Carole has also bred and trained for competition American Saddlebred, Morgan, and Arabian horses. Both her horses and the riders she has trained have excelled in winning an abundance of honors. *Livery to Lipizzans* is Carole's forthcoming book.

In retirement, Carole continues to love *horsepower*. Missing the challenge of competition, she trained as a NASCAR driver, and drove a bright red *Dale Earnhardt, Jr.* supercharged Monte Carlo. She raced her Honda S2000 throughout the Midwest. Today, Carole drives a roaring hyper-blue metallic Camaro SS, and is still remembered on the Iowa race car circuit as a "fast woman."

Saraff

Are *good* horses born that way, or are they made? In the 1970s the owner of a black and white American Paint mare, bred her to an Egyptian Arabian stallion, hoping to have a black and white foal to compete with in the future. However, the foal was born with the color of his sire, which was chestnut with white mane and tail. The disappointed owner quickly sold the colt. They did, however, do him the great service of naming him *Saraff*, the Egyptian word for "beautiful".

The new owner turned Saraff out with an appaloosa and a pony, and proceeded to neglect the young colt for the next year and a half. Being a youngster, he was at the bottom of the pecking order, and was never able to eat enough to help his growing body thrive. He managed to stay alive by eating the scrub brush and weeds in the pasture, but he grew thinner daily.

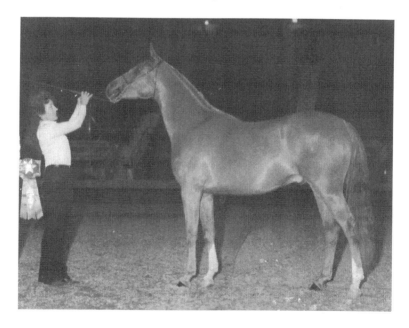

In December of that year, I heard about this colt starving not far from my stable. I drove to see him, and found him in extremely poor condition. I bought him and transported him to my stable that same day. This colt was just one of many horses that I had "rescued" over the years, and they had all survived and done well. However, my veterinarian took one look at this colt and pronounced that I wouldn't be able to save this youngster, he was too far gone. The open sores that were all along his back, down all four legs, on both ears and down the front of his face, were signs of one of the last stages of severe malnutrition. His skin was dying.

I decided to do all in my power to make what might be his last days or months as comfortable as possible. Every day I carefully fed the colt numerous feedings of small amounts of good feed, and rubbed ointment into all his open sores. One month later, he was still alive, so my veterinarian decided we might be able to start a monthly worming program, which would help him gain weight, if the wormer didn't kill him. That was actually just what Saraff needed, and after eliminating the worms that were robbing his body of nutrients, he began to look better each month.

By the next summer, when he turned three years old, he was doing well enough that I started his training under saddle. He seemed to appreciate this new home that fed him so well! He acted as if he thought a rider on his back was easy work and even fun!

When he shed his winter hair in the spring of his fourth year, we were amazed to see a brilliant shiny chestnut coat, set off by an almost white mane and tail. He looked like an entirely different horse from the starving colt that came to us. His body was now well muscled with that beautiful Arabian head, and large expressive eyes.

Saraff's training came along so easily, that I took him to the large Detroit Arabian show. What a wonderful surprise when he won the Blue Ribbon in his Halter Class. As a novice performer, he also won Green Hunter Under Saddle. He placed in three other Dressage classes. I was amazed to see how this horse performed like an old veteran, at his very first horse show. I could see his potential as my next National Champion Dressage Horse!

But fate took a cruel turn, and Saraff injured an eye while out in a paddock for exercise. After a week at Michigan State University Veterinary Medical Center, and many weeks of care, the eye was not able to be saved. At that time, an Arabian with a blind eye could not be shown in competition. His show career abruptly ended.

But by that time, I was so fond of this horse who seemed so anxious to please, that I decided he would never be sold. He would stay with me for the rest of his life as a lesson horse. He slipped into that role just as easily, and began to be the lesson horse of choice for all my students.

Saraff became equally at home giving dressage, jumping, English, or Western Pleasure lessons. During this time, I started to teach him a few tricks. He loved to "shake hands" with people he was introduced to, count or add numbers, and waltz to music.

In the late 1980s, we began to use Saraff as a vaulting horse, and he was just as steady and reliable with children running and jumping onto his back, doing handstands, forming pyramids on his back, or riding Roman-style, standing on his back.

During the 1990s, Saraff was used for exhibitions for disabled people in wheelchairs, and for handicapped children. He seemed to thrive on all the attention, and loved visiting each person in wheelchairs. Saraff even acted in a Nativity play, acting the part of the donkey, carrying Mary (bareback and sidesaddle) toward Bethlehem.

I'd like to think that my training made Saraff the wonderful, kind, exceptional horse that he was, but it must have been more than that. It must have been his genes, and bloodlines just "clicked" to give him that "blessed temperament". And perhaps horses really *do* feel appreciation when they are rescued. It was my honor to be able to share twenty-seven years with this magnificent and lovable animal. In January of 2015, at the age of twenty-nine, Saraff suffered a heart attack and passed away. He died the way he had lived his life, a gentleman to the end.

Saraff is the only horse buried in the backyard of my home in Cedar Rapids. He was cremated and then buried in a little cemetery with the remains of all the dogs and cats that have shared my life, my parents' life, and my grandparents' life here on this long-ago farm, now just a small acreage. My first and second horse lived here in the 1950s, and now, sixty-four years later, my last horse will remain here for eternity.

Quiet Perseverance

Walking down the long aisle through the horse stable, I could not help but notice the apprehensive, worried looks on each horse as they watched me walk closer to their stalls. The racket coming from the last stall of the stable was enough to make anyone cringe in fear. The surprise, when I reached that last stall, was seeing one of the most majestic white horses I had ever seen. My past twenty years had been spent raising and training horses for competition, but this horse's spectacular beauty held me spellbound, even as he was rearing, striking the bars that held him with his front hooves, and kicking almost non-stop at the oak walls. To add to the din was his nightmarish screams, high-pitched stallion "threats" to anyone that might dare come close.

The owners of the stable had asked me to take this horse, known as "Killer" to my stable, to train him enough to sell. They told me that that electric shocks and beatings with baseball bats had not made this horse manageable. Looking at this "beast" trying to dismantle his stall board by board didn't even make me think twice. I could see immediately what was creating the madness in this horse; the stall had been "electrified" with hot wire. The constant shocks, in the stall he thought of as his "home" were driving him insane. I knew I had to give this beautiful animal another chance at life. If he was found to truly be an "outlaw" and was untrainable, I also knew he would have to be euthanized.

The next week, when he was to be delivered to my stable, we could hear his arrival long before the truck and trailer drove into view. We could hear him kicking and screaming, and as they came closer, we could see the horse trailer rocking and lurching up and down, forward and back. It took two handlers to lead him to the barn, one had a chain over his nose, the other with a chain under his chin. He came most of the way on his hind legs, flailing out at each of his handlers.

Before the owners left, they gave me a list of things that could NOT be done with this difficult horse; giving a bath, putting a bridle on over his ears, or using electric clippers. The stout young lady that worked for me, Sandy, looked at the list and said, "Well, I know what we're going to be doing all day today!" And, she was right.

My life training horses had given me a lot of experience with "difficult" horses, but my first European instructor instilled in me the one theory that always works, "quiet perseverance". I also had experience with a horse that truly was a "man-eater", and would try to kill humans, so I knew enough to try to protect myself during the first encounter with "Killer".

Our beginning lesson that day would be for me to enter the horse's stall and try to groom him with a brush and curry, to establish some sort of relationship that did not include electric shocks. Then, if possible, I would try to put a bridle on his head. One thing I had learned from my Veterinarian was to have a good, strong person in the doorway of the stall, holding a spade... a pointed shovel... with the instructions to "cave in the horse's head with the shovel, if he grabbed me with his teeth."

Holding onto Killer's halter, I began brushing in my "quiet perseverance" method. He jerked me up and down and all around the stall, but I held on and quietly kept brushing. His ears flicked back and forth as he wondered what this new human technique was that actually felt good!

Putting the bridle on over his ears turned out to be as challenging as the owners had warned. I made the bridle as large as possible, and proceeded with quiet determination to slip it onto his head. Once again, Killer lifted me off the ground by rearing and striking out. I managed to maintain my hold on his halter, and to keep my body close to his shoulder. After a few minutes of being tossed around like a rag doll, I was still beside him, holding his halter, and trying to slide the bridle over his ears. Assistant Sandy patiently stood in the doorway, shovel at the ready, but so far no direct attacks toward me. After a few minutes of rebelling, Killer gave a big sigh, and let me put the bridle over his ears. Sandy and I smiled at each other. This was an intelligent horse! Evidently, I was the first person that didn't run from him when he stood on his hind legs, and I also didn't abuse him with a whip, baseball bat or electric shocks. I carefully slipped the bridle off of his head, being very careful not to hurt his ears.

We then led the horse to my wash rack. I brushed and groomed him again, and then turned on the electric clippers. Once again, he began rearing, striking and fighting for a minute or so, but then, giving a big sigh, he let me clip a few long hairs from under his chin and around his front ankles. Another success! I then turned on the warm water hose and let some water trickle around his feet. This time he only fought for about 30 seconds, then gave up and stood quietly for a quick bath.

Sandy and I were ecstatic. This was indeed a very intelligent horse! I reached into my pocket for a piece of carrot and offered it to the worried stallion. At first, he shied away from my open palm with the carrot, but then cautiously sniffed at my hand, and gently took the treat. I petted him a bit more over all his body, and then Sandy and I put Killer back into his new home, a stall with no electric wires, but lots of good hay and treats. We knew that by tomorrow, we had to have a new name for this horse!

That evening, looking at this wild horse's registration papers, I was shocked. This beautiful stallion was a registered purebred Lipizzan, whose parents had been imported from Austria. His registered name was Pluto Bona II. I decided then, that we could call him "Beau", because I was sure he would eventually become a gentleman under saddle! I also made the decision to buy him and train him for myself; he was never going to be for sale!

I knew that retraining this horse might take twice as long as starting a young horse from scratch. The Lipizzan stallion called "Killer" by his previous owners had surprised me many times in this first day by showing me he was indeed open to new training methods. Now, to erase bad habits and/or bad memories, I needed to go back to basics.

Changing the horse's name from Killer to Beau helped all of us in my stable view him in a kinder light. The first day had proved that Beau was very capable of learning, and he did not seem to even think about attacking us, so we proceeded to remodel his mindset under saddle.

With a rubber bit in his mouth and the saddle in place, I attached a long line to the bit and asked him to walk around me in a large circle. My aim was to perfect the cues for walk, trot, canter, and whoa.

Suddenly things went in a totally different direction! When I pointed the whip behind Beau's hind legs to ask him to go forward, he immediately stopped. Waving the whip a little behind him to urge him on, created an even more unusual response. Beau gathered himself like a coiled spring and lifted his front legs off the ground in Levade. At this moment, I wasn't sure if he was rebelling at my basic commands or making things up as he went along.

Popping the whip behind Beau then created the biggest surprise of all! Beau leaped up into the air, kicking backwards in what is called Capriole, a move that was taught to horses back in the days of hand-to-hand combat with soldiers carrying swords. The Capriole was used when the rider was surrounded by the enemy. You can imagine that a 1,000 lb. horse leaping high into the air and kicking out behind would cause the enemy soldiers to back away quickly.

Well, I thought it was time for a different approach to find if this horse even knew the basics, so I tried pointing the whip toward his front shoulder to see if I could move him out away from me and make him walk or trot forward. That didn't work either! The minute the whip was near his front legs, Beau bowed, both knees down on the ground!

I began to get the idea then that this horse had been taught, sometime in his first eight years, a serious of circus tricks! I was going to have to adjust my training methods to work with this horse's idea of what was expected.

I asked my assistant trainer to come to the arena. I had her hold Beau's head while I carefully mounted, not sure what was going to happen next. I wanted to keep him on that long line as a safety measure, hoping the second human could help me stop him if things got too wild and out of control.

Sandy pointed the whip behind Beau, and I "clucked" and squeezed my legs against his sides, asking him to walk forward. Up in the air we went. I tapped him with the short riding whip I carried, and he leaped high into the air, forcefully kicking out with his hind legs. My first Capriole under saddle! That was an extremely powerful feeling I had never experienced before on a horse!

I tried tapping Beau on the shoulder with my whip, hoping we could just walk forward. Oh no, now he's bowing, and I had to lean back to keep from falling over his neck and head.

This wasn't working at all. We had to try something else! I had Sandy remove the long line, and almost immediately Beau's demeanor changed. As soon as she walked away, he started walking forward and allowing me to practice turning with the reins, stopping on "whoa" and backing up. From there, his daily training progressed. Evidently, the tricks were only done on a long line!

I later learned that Beau's first trainer had worked for Barnum & Bailey Circus, and was famous for teaching horses all sorts of unusual tricks. Sadly, when that trainer later sold Beau, no instructions went with him to the new owners, and Beau's life went downhill from there. The new family did not understand that Beau was doing exactly what he had been taught. They thought all these unusual movements were signs of rebelling and fighting back at his handlers.

Since I had been training all breeds of horses for over twenty years—mostly Saddlebreds, Arabians, and Morgans—it took only these few days to discover that this Lipizzan was *the* most intelligent *and* the most athletic horse I had ever ridden! His training progressed so quickly that I began to think that he stayed up at night reading the Austrian book, *Complete Training of Horse and Rider*! Any movement I tried to teach him came *so easily*. The compact Lipizzan, whose hind legs work under the body, make the lateral and collection movements effortless the first time they try. Each day using "quiet determination" saw progress, and it didn't take long for me to decide that if all Lipizzans were as talented as Beau, then I would be on a quest to find the best Lipizzan mares I could afford, and build a breeding program around him.

With steady daily practice, in only a few months Beau had perfected doing all the normal gaits with me. He and I began doing musical exhibitions in Michigan and around the Midwest. He was a spectacular pure white horse, with a lot of bounce in his trot that thrilled the crowds. Beau was so athletic that he had learned easily and quickly to do the lateral movements, trotting forward and sideways at the same time. He also developed a wonderful Piaffe, a trot in place, and a beautiful Passage, a trot that is hesitant and elevated. Beau ended our exhibitions with the Levade, standing on his hind legs while tucking his front legs under his chest. During the applause, he would bow. Now we did all these maneuvers together, similar to the flowing movements of a pair of ice skaters. Beau had two favorite musical pieces that he enjoyed... the *2001 Space Odyssey* and the President's *Hail to the Chief*. When he heard these begin to play over the sound system, he would start to Passage into the arena all on his own. I always struggled to keep up with this super-intelligent and athletic horse!

Over the next five years, I searched for, and purchased, the best Lipizzan mares in this country. Beau and I together went on to create some of the most magnificent Lipizzan horses in the USA for competition. Beau became the most mild-mannered stallion I had ever handled. He was a joy to breed to mares and to ride in exhibitions. Beau died in his 25th year on my farm, surrounded by his thirty broodmares and his many offspring. This "killer" horse had become my Guardian Angel. I look forward to spending eternity with him in Heaven.

Carole Michalek Gauger

NASCAR Race School

Michigan International Speedway

Michigan International Speedway can be an intimidating place, even on a quiet day. I had attended NASCAR races at the track in previous years. It was always amazing to see Brooklyn, Michigan, a town of 1,200 people, transformed into a madhouse of people and cars and RVs of every size and description for miles in every direction surrounding the track on race days. My visit today was going to be totally different from a normal NASCAR race weekend. This weekend I was going to be driving a race car on that huge two-mile, highly banked track! It was thrilling to me, just to drive into Brooklyn, and see the mammoth facility that loomed ahead of me. I drove around the outside of the track, until I came to the "Tunnel Gate." I wanted to see where I would be entering the infield the next morning!

It had taken me all day to drive from Cedar Rapids, Iowa, to the Michigan speedway, but I stopped my Camaro long enough to take a picture of my car at the entrance to "Tunnel Gate," before driving on to my motel for the evening. I ate a light meal of fast food, before turning in and trying to sleep. I knew it was going to be hard to relax and sleep, because I was very excited to think about driving one of the 700 hp NASCAR racers the next day! This was something I had eagerly anticipated for many months since signing up for the "Racer's Introduction Class". Even though, years ago, back in the 1950s, my first car had been somewhat of a "hot rod". I had participated in drag races at the Cordova International Raceway in Illinois in those teenage years. That was over fifty years before! In the meantime, I had married, raised two children, and had a very serious job that required that I drive a pick-up truck. Now, here I was, newly retired, and about to attempt to control an extremely fast race car on a track! And I couldn't wait!!!

At 7am I excitedly drove my Camaro through the now-open, very tall and wide Tunnel Gate, under the racetrack, and out onto the infield. I saw a cluster of cars and groups of people—mostly men—standing in front of one of the low concrete buildings. Parking my car among the rest, I went to stand with the others. No one spoke to me, and that was fine. I was almost too nervous to try to carry on a conversation with strangers.

At 7:30am the doors opened. We were directed into one of two lines: Drivers or Spectators. Almost immediately, the women and men separated. Women lined up as spectators, and all of the men lined up in the driver's line.

It didn't take more than a few seconds, until some of the men turned to me and said, "I think you're in the wrong line." Of course, I wasn't! I was in the driver's line, and proud of it, even though a bit intimidated. I was not only the sole woman in that line, but at age 62, I was obviously the oldest person in that line!

The secretaries at the check-in desk said they were thrilled to see a woman signing up to drive in the race school! After signing liability waivers, we were shuttled into another room and fitted with a fireproof racing suit and helmet. There was a problem finding sizes small enough to fit me. I was so excited to be a driver, that I didn't even mind that the orange suit I was given was at least two or three sizes too large!

The first two hours we sat in a classroom listening to our instructor, Sean Christy, who was young, tall, thin, and handsome! His first written instruction on the blackboard was in large capital letters:

S M O O O O O O O T H!!! SMOOTH!!

He repeated over and over that at the speed we would be going, we did NOT want to ask the car to make any sudden adjustments! Driving smoothly was driving safely! He taught us about the layout of the track, and the protocol of cars entering or leaving Pit Road, and the seven reference points we would need to memorize to safely enter and exit each of the left-hand turns on the high-banked oval. He emphatically stated that there would be no downshifting, and no speed shifting. He did burst my "need for speed" when he told us there was a governor on each car to keep us under 160mph. I had been hoping to drive near 200mph as the NASCAR racers did on this five-lane-wide track. Oh well, I guess I could be satisfied with only 160 since all of us were novices!

We were then herded into vans, seven apprehensive students and one instructor. They drove us out onto Pit Road, where the pit crews waited to work on the cars. The instructor demonstrated how to enter and exit from the pits. He then picked up speed, to show us we needed to be going at least 100mph by the end of Pit Road to merge into the existing traffic. I knew that professional NASCAR drivers might be practicing with their cars at close to 200mph. The instructor pointed out each of the seven reference points we were going to need to look for to enter each turn, how to find the mid-point of the turn, and then how to exit the turn toward the next reference point. This would ensure the fastest and safest line for the car.

After that drive, we were allowed to jump into our own cars and then meet on Pit Road. This time we each had an instructor ride with us, to practice passing and being passed. This adventure was already TOO SLOW for me, as we were not allowed to go over 70mph on that trip! Seventy in my Camaro, on that huge, wide track, felt as if I could have walked faster!

After a break, and leaving our cars in the parking lot once again, we were each introduced to our pit crew. I had three young men, and the team leader, Steve. They had a special car chosen for me, the only one with the seat close enough to the steering wheel, to enable me to reach the gas and brake pedals. It was Jeff Burton's #99 car, so he must be a very small man!

We donned the fire suits, the neck braces, and the helmet. It was a good thing I had practiced crawling in through the window of my Camaro at home in my driveway, because that's the only way to enter these race cars! My crew started to help me through the window, but I insisted, "I can do this!", and I did. Once in place, Steve leaned in to fasten my five-point seat belts, and show me how to fire up the big engine. Oh boy, was it loud inside there! Steve had to yell to make himself heard. He told me we had to sit there and let the engine warm up to 160 degrees before starting our first run of eight laps.

The first five cars lined up on Pit Road ahead of my #99 roared to life. They started for the track. One of the men obviously stomped on the gas a bit too hard, because I saw his car fishtailing all the way down Pit Road.

Steve yelled in my ear, "I don't want you to do that!"

That was fine with me, I didn't want to feel a car this powerful a little out of control while close to the Pit Road cement walls! They were only sending out five cars at a time during this first practice.

Then it was my turn. My memory of that first eight laps is a bit fuzzy. I just remember being careful to ease the car through the gears without spinning the tires, and without fishtailing, and being sure to reach 100mph by the end of Pit Road. Then I had to concentrate on working my way up the track to merge with other traffic... except there wasn't any! The first five cars had finished their eight laps, and they were back in their pit stalls.

After my eight laps, Steve and my pit crew were extremely happy with my performance. I think they were worried that an older lady like me might embarrass them! They said I had an average speed for the sixteen miles of just over 103. They thought that was great, I thought that was WAY too slow! There were spotters on the roof of the grandstand with binoculars, watching each of the novice drivers, and ready to "black flag" anyone that they thought could not handle the speed of the car and the turns. I was determined that was not going to happen to me!

The next time out, we were allowed to go 10 laps, and I passed one car, and that was a thrill in itself! I don't know who I passed, I was too busy having fun. That time I had an average speed of 120.

By this time, my pit crew and Steve were singing my praises to the other teams, although I didn't know this at the time. The last race of the day, we would be driving forty laps (eighty miles).

Steve told me, "Go for it! You can do this! Don't even bother to get off the gas on the turns! This car is set up to take the turns at 200mph, and we know you can handle this, so keep your foot in the gas the entire forty laps!" I remember thinking, "Really????"

The green flag dropped, and I was off. All my teenage years of shifting at speed came back to me, and I was really "off to the races." I put the pedal to the metal, and concentrated on those reference points to get into each turn and out as smoothly as possible. Every turn of the steering wheel causes loss of RPM, so I was determined to be as smooth as possible. This forty laps went by too quickly, but I remember just having a big smile and feeling filled to the brim with JOY every second. I was only passed once, and it was by my instructor, Sean, but it took him half the track to get by me! I was really into the racing spirit by then!

Steve had told me that on this particular race track, as I entered each turn at 160, if I lightly lifted my hands off the steering wheel, the car would find the best groove on the banked curve to take the turn. That was almost frightening, but I believed him, and found it was true! What a rush of pure adrenalin when it all feels just right, and you're one with the car! That time the timers told me I averaged 150, which included my leaving and reentering the pits, so knew I was at 160 most of the time!

After shakily climbing out of the car, and posing for some pictures, we drivers stood around and talked for a few minutes. One of the men admitted he was terrified the entire time, and had been told he had earned the nickname "turtle" for being the slowest on the track. His face was bright red, and he was sweating profusely. I felt sorry for him, because I had found it such great fun!

The wives and girlfriends then came running to congratulate their mates, and off we all went our separate ways. Of course, I was alone, by my choice. I wanted to attend this school without any family or friends, just in case I failed. But being alone that evening was difficult. I drove back to the motel "WIRED". I was SO up, so filled with adrenalin, I just wanted to share my experiences with someone! I called my son, my daughter, and two good friends but no one was home to answer their phones! I probably left some disjointed messages, but I couldn't sleep, couldn't eat, couldn't watch TV or read.... I felt I was still on the track at 160mph, with the tall wire fence flying by the right side of the car.

I finally slept four hours, ate a hearty breakfast, and was back at the track by 7:30am. Our pit crews were ready, and we were being prepped for a full day of racing.

First we were to drive onto the track and pretend it was a real race. We were to pass whenever possible, and allow ourselves to be passed if a faster car came up on our rear bumper. Today I had a new race car that fit me well.

They told me that it was the Dale Earnhardt, Jr. #8 car! I was thrilled! Dale and the #8 car were one of my favorites, of course. I hoped this car was going to be even faster!

Off we went for forty laps. I still tried to be as smooth as possible, even though I was pushing that car for all it was worth. My foot was so forceful on that gas pedal that I thought I might be pushing it through the floorboard. I wanted to go faster! I was disappointed that all through our pretend race, I never had a chance to pass anyone else, and no one ever passed me. As I pulled back into Pit Road, I was getting madder by the minute.

After crawling out the window, I yelled at Steve, "You sent me out there alone! Just because I'm a woman and older, you thought I couldn't handle a real race car?"

Steve and the crew were all laughing until Steve calmed me down by saying, "You weren't out there alone! You were so far ahead of all the others, you couldn't even see them in your rear-view mirror!"

Suddenly I was surrounded by the secretaries from the office. They all wanted to see this woman that was "setting new track records" and beating all the men! That made my day, my month, and my year! Retiring and finding a new hobby was turning out to be great experience.

The last race of the day I was set up to race my instructor, Sean, just the two of us. Steve and my crew excitedly told me to PLEASE beat Sean, because he's known to be a real chauvinist, and hates having women in his race school. They knew I was certainly going to try! I assumed, however, that he did NOT have a governor on his car, and could go over 160 if he wanted.

Soon we were buckled in. The heat from the engine was baking me in the race suit, and the noise was assaulting my ears. But oh, what a great sound! And we were OFF! The forty laps went by quickly, with Sean and

I trading places many times, passing each other on the low side, or the high side, whichever worked the best. As we came around the final Turn Four, headed for the checkered flag, Sean was below me on the low side. I started easing the nose of my car down lower and lower, forcing him down to the apron as we screamed past the waving checkered flag! I looked over, and my pit crew was jumping over the wall, leaping up and down and shouting for joy! Once more around the track to slow down enough to enter Pit Road, and while everyone was congratulating me, Sean came storming down the track from his car. He appeared really mad.

I tried to tease him a little and say, "Oh, come on, Sean, you let me win, just to be a good sport."

"I did not!" He yelled. "You were going to run me off the track!"

Well, I could not tell a lie; yes, I was!

John Boswell Hudson

John shares memories of childhood summers spent on his grandparents farm in northeast Missouri in the 1930s. Those were the days of true horse power, in which teams of horses and manly brawn extracted a livelihood from the pastures and fields of a 160-acre homestead. It was before rural electrification, and before World War II changed the world.

John was the perfect age for farm fun and adventure: old enough to remember the experience, yet too young to participate in the hard work. For some readers John's recollections will rekindle old memories; for others, his stories will open a door to a vanished way of life.

Barefoot on the Farm

Our shoes come off as soon as we arrive at the farm and change clothes. My sister Helen and I go barefoot all summer. Our feet are tender for the first few days, but soon the bottoms of our feet grow tough, and we run everywhere barefooted. We just are careful where we put our feet. We manage to miss the cow pies, and the horses are not a problem. Chickens are everywhere in the barnyard, so we frequently have to clean our feet with a twig between our toes, or by rubbing our feet across a patch of dirt. Grandad keeps the yard fenced, so we don't need to clean our feet if we stay in the yard. I like the feel of the cool, soft grass on the bottom of my feet.

Supper is the evening meal on the farm, and tonight consists of leftovers from noon dinner: cold fried chicken, corn bread, fresh lima beans, milk from Grandad's Jersey cows, and for dessert, Grandma's homemade apple pie.

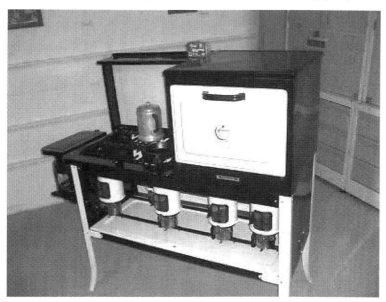

Kaleidoscope

We sit at a long table on the screened porch, comfortable in the heat of the Midwestern summer. Grandma does most of her cooking in the summer kitchen, which has a kerosene stove at one end of the porch. In the hot summer weather of Missouri this is cooler than using the large black wood stove in the kitchen. Nearby is the ice box with handsome dark wooden doors. A large block of ice that the ice man delivered the day before goes in the top right space. Inside the bottom door is a bucket to catch the water from the melting ice. The large compartment on the left is the place for keeping food cold so it won't spoil.

Evening

As the day turns to dusk, Grandad strikes a match and lights the wicks of several kerosene lamps, carefully adjusting their wicks high enough to cast enough light, but low enough so the flame does not smoke and dirty their glass chimneys.

He walks into the dining room and lights the Aladdin lamp, which is my favorite. This has a glass base and a glass reservoir containing coal oil, which is what we call kerosene. The lamp has a circular wick, called a "mantle," that burns very bright, with a slender glass chimney which fits around the burning mantle and is as tall as my arm from my elbow to my hand. There is no need to pump the kerosene reservoir. The Aladdin lamp is very handsome, and it seems quite mysterious and wonderful.

Grandad sits down in his chair by the dining table, puts on his reading glasses, and picks up his copy of the *Edina Sentinel* weekly newspaper. The comics are printed on green paper, and that's the part of the newspaper I like. Sometimes Grandad listens to his battery-powered radio after he finishes reading the paper.

It is soon bedtime, and we go to the living room and open the hide-a-bed sofa, covered in black horsehair. My sister Helen sleeps there, and I sleep on the wide shelf in the bay window. On hot, muggy Missouri nights, any breeze is wonderful to feel, and all the windows and doors are open to catch any breath of air.

Screens keep out the insects, of which there are plenty on the farm. As I drift off to sleep, I can dimly see the framed photographs of family members on the several tables in the room.

Dragging the Road

When it rains, the dusty dirt roads in the neighborhood became muddy and impassable for most cars.

Grandad's Model T could often get through the mud because it has high clearance, leaving deep ruts in the road. After the rain stops and the roads dry out, the ruts are left hard-baked in the clay of the road.

Grandad hitches the team to the drag, which is a wooden box about 3 feet long and 6 feet wide. The box is upside down with large rocks on top to weight it down, and it has a steel blade fastened on the front to scrape the dirt road. Grandad walks alongside the drag holding the reins to guide the horses, and I tag alongside. I like watching the steel blade cut into the dried clay as it scrapes the dirt into the ruts, making the road smooth again. It's always a treat to go along with Grandad when he drags the road.

Each farmer in the neighborhood drags his part of the road that runs past his farm. Not all farmers get their roads dragged as soon as they should after a rain.

If my sister and I are riding with Grandad in his Model T and we see ruts in the road, we plead, "Grandad, drive in the ruts. Please, Grandad, drive in the ruts," until he finally agrees. Grandad carefully steers the tires into the crooked ruts, and the car careens wildly from side-to-side as Grandad drives down the road, Helen and I laughing all the way. Grandad doesn't do it very often because he says it isn't good for the car, so we have to be content with only the occasional treat.

The Hayfield

Grandad's farm uses real horsepower, as well as manual labor. Grandad has four horses so that he can rest one team while working the other. These big draft horses tower over me when I stand beside them to pet them or feed them a treat. They have big feet—they seem as big as pie plates—much bigger than the hooves of Grandad's riding horse. They are well trained and gentle. Grandad sometimes puts me on the back of one of the horses, and it feels pretty high from up there.

Standing in the hay field, I watch as Grandad rides by on his two-wheeled mower, with its long sickle reaching out to the right, Grandad riding upright on the metal seat with its drain holes, holding the reins of the team of horses. I admire my grandfather, with his leather-tanned face, his straw hat worn to shield the sun, his blue work shirt tucked into his overalls, his shirt sleeves rolled up just above his elbows, exposing his arms dark-tanned by years of working in the sun. I wear my blue work shirt and overalls exactly the same way. I have my own straw hat, too.

I take a deep breath in the field of new-mown timothy hay, the fragrance filling my nose as I hold a stem in my hand, admiring the soft texture of the long symmetrical head, green-yellow in the forenoon light of the sun. Timothy is the hay to grow if you have horses, and I've always liked it. I sometimes pick my teeth with the stem, and I savor the sweet taste when I chew it. I am at that perfect age, old enough to be aware of what is going on, but too young to help with the hard work, so I spend my time watching and staying out of the way. Grandad is very strict about that—staying out of harm's way.

As Grandad drives the mower, the tall hay falls gracefully upon the ground, waiting to be raked into windrows.

Later, after the cut hay has partially dried, Grandad hitches the team to his sulky rake, and rides back and forth across the hay field. I like the sulky rake, with its long, curved steel teeth sweeping in a graceful arc behind the sulky. These teeth gather the loose hay as Grandad guides the horses across the hayfield. When the rake is full of hay, Grandad pulls a lever that raises the teeth, and hay is left behind in a wide pile.

He drops several piles as he crosses the field. Coming back the other way, he drops hay from the rake next to the previous piles. By the time he finishes going back and forth across the field, the hay lies in long parallel rows from one end of the field to the other. This process fascinates me. I admire the pattern in the field.

Bringing in the Hay

When the hay in these windrows has dried completely, several neighboring farmers come to help bring in the hay.

The creak of leather harness and the jangle of chain resonate like music as the horses pull the hay wagon, leaning into their horse collars with the traces tight against the oak singletrees, weathered silver-gray by rain and sun. The wagon has four steel wheels and a flat bed with several stakes fastened at the sides and ends to hold the loose hay. Grandad slowly drives the team of horses along the windrows that lie across the hay field like fragrant ribbons.

Kaleidoscope

Several men in their blue shirts and overalls pitch the hay from the ground onto the wagon with their pitchforks. The long wooden handles of the pitchforks, polished by years of working hands sliding along their surfaces, end in three or four sharp steel prongs, kept shiny by the constant pitching of the hay. A man standing on the wagon is working the growing pile of hay to keep it evenly distributed across the wagon. It is hot and dusty work. The red handkerchiefs of the men are damp with sweat in the humidity of the summer heat. Every now and then one of the farmers takes a drink of cool water from a ceramic jug covered with damp burlap. The jug is sitting under a shady tree near the barbed-wire fence at the edge of the hayfield.

"Grandad, why is the jug covered with wet burlap?" I ask.

"Well, Cap, the moisture in the burlap slowly evaporates, and the evaporation absorbs heat, so the water keeps cool."

"Grandad, you sure do know a lot of things."

"It's always a good thing to know the things that make life easier," he replies.

I taste the cool water. It is June, and the summer will get hotter.

"Grandad, this water sure is good on a hot day."

When the hay wagon is full, the man on top jumps to the ground and walks alongside with the other men. Grandad drives the wagon across the field through the gateway into the barnyard.

The Hayloft

Putting the loose hay in the hayloft of the barn is one of the most intriguing operations of all to a small boy from the city. I have always been fascinated by how mechanical things work. Grandad stops the horses so the wagon is directly under the open door in the second floor of the red barn. Normally this door is kept shut, but today the door is hanging down against the side of the barn, open wide so that the hay can be moved into the second-floor hayloft that is open to the rafters.

A track for the hay trolley is attached to the underside of the ridgepole that runs the full length of the barn. The track projects out through the barn door ending directly over the hay wagon below. A triangular piece of the barn roof projects out over the end of the track to protect it from rain. The hayfork is hanging from a rope that runs up to a pulley in the trolley above. Then the rope runs across the barn just under the track, through a small window at the opposite end of the barn, through a pulley and down the side of the barn, through another pulley, and the rope is finally fastened to a singletree harnessed to a horse. My older cousin, Dick, who lives on the adjoining farm, stands at the horse's head, holding the lead rope fastened to the horse's halter.

Grandad climbs up on the wagon and grabs a dangling trip line and pulls down the hayfork, which is U-shaped and almost as tall as I am. It has small retractable blades near the pointed ends that hold the hay from slipping off. As Dick waits, Grandad forces the hayfork firmly into the piled hay. Then he hollers to Dick, who slowly leads the horse away from the far side of the barn, pulling the rope that lifts the loaded hayfork slowly into the air.

Standing by the wagon and looking up, I watch with concentration as the hayfork latches onto the trolley, and then begins rolling into the hayloft along the track, until the load of hay reaches the waiting men. One of the men pulls the trip rope, retracting the blades, and the hay slides off the fork. The men then use their pitchforks to toss the hay against the walls to make room for the next load of hay.

After watching outside for a while, I walk into the dim interior of the barn—a passageway between the horse stalls and the grain bins—and climb the ladder to the hayloft. The worn rungs of the wooden ladder are smooth to my hands as I climb up through the square hole into the hayloft, where I watch the men pitching the hay.

The summer sunlight filters in through the small window at the rear of the barn, and through the large open door at the front, granting entry to the daylight and to fresh air. Even with the large door open, the loft is a dim, hot, and dusty place.

As Dick leads the horse back to the side of the barn, the men in the hayloft pull the trolley with the hayfork back to the end of the track outside the large door, and Grandad grabs the dangling trip line to pull down the hayfork, which he shoves into the remaining hay.

The entire operation is repeated until the hay wagon is empty. Then Grandad drives the wagon out to the hayfield for another load of hay, and this goes on until the hayloft is full.

Once one of those big draft horses with very large hoofs stepped on Dick's foot, and it was painful. He got to take the rest of the day off. Uncle Rich did not make a fuss or take Dick to the doctor—after all, this was a farm—and Dick was still able to walk, although carefully. After a few days his foot recovered and no more was said about it. People in the Midwest take these things as a matter of course. They don't complain or go to the doctor.

John Boswell Hudson

Grandma's Gooseberry Pie

Grandma has several gooseberry bushes, and I some-times eat them right off the bush. They are sour and make my mouth feel like I am sucking a lemon.

But the thing I like the most about gooseberries is—yummy gooseberry pie!

There is nothing, nor has there ever been, a pie as delicious, with so delectable a crust, with a filling as mouth-watering, as my grandmother's homemade gooseberry pie. The golden-brown crust, gently curving with its little holes to let out the steam, its outer edge pinched into dimples around the edge of the pie dish, is inviting me to taste. The flavor and texture of the crust—made with lard—is flaky, yet with a slight chewy texture. But then there is the flavor and texture of the bottom crust, with its ever-so-slight suggestion of raw pie dough—not that it's undercooked, just not completely dry.

The gooseberry filling, tart but sweetened with just the right amount of sugar, with a bit of flour sifted in, consists of a gooey, wonderfully delicious, mouth-filling flood tide of flavor, which when commingled with the taste of the crust, fills me with pure bliss.

I once saw a magazine cartoon that illustrates my feeling for Grandma's gooseberry pie. A couple walking along a sidewalk pass by a café. Displayed in the window are three signs.

The first sign says:

Pie slice, $1.00

The second sign says:

Pie like Grandma made, $2.00

The third sign says:

Pie like you *remember* Grandma made, $3.00

Sandra Cermak Hudson

Sandra's stories take place during a golden age for childhood. It was a time when children could safely roam and explore far and wide.

There were few commercial toys. Children, even toddlers, learned to create their own amusements from everyday items found at home or in their neighborhood.

It was a time before organized after-school sports. Boys and girls, from six to sixteen, gathered on school playgrounds and in vacant lots to invent and shape their own games. Older kids mentored and looked out for the younger ones.

World War II was raging across Europe, North Africa, and in the Pacific, influencing our play, and instilling a strong sense of community and neighborliness.

Herein Sandra shares stories from her forthcoming book *Czech Childhood: Cedar Rapids, Iowa 1938-1946*

Big Bohemie

"Hunka Ted's a big Bohemie, Hunka Ted's a big Bohemie." Ocie Allen circled his uncle like a ball on a tether, waiting to be snatched in and given a friendly wallop, a knuckle rub, or the ultimate reward, a tickle. When the tickles came, we kids would giggle so hard we'd nearly pee our pants. On this warm October day in 1938, I shadowed my seven-year old cousin's every move. I too circled my father shouting, "Hunka Ted's a big Bohemie".

My Dad tired of the game long before we did. He grabbed me, swung me around his head a time or two, and sat me on his shoulders with my legs straddling his neck. Then he quickly reached down, wrapped his arm around Ocie's waist, shackled the kicking screaming whirlwind to his hip, and began spinning around the yard like a top.

Ocie yowled. I tightened my knees into Dad's neck and clinched my fingers through his curly red hair, grasping as tight as a nearly four-year old could. My body arched back with centrifugal force and my long finger curls whipped my face. The view around me began to blur. I squealed with delight. When we were properly dizzy, Dad deposited us on the front porch glider, gave it a strong push, and retreated into the house, leaving us to recover in the glider's gentle swinging motion.

Ocie recuperated first. He slid off the glider and pulled at the handle of the screen door. It was locked. He yelled through the screen: "Hunka Ted's a big Bohemie." Again, I mimicked his every move. We chanted and banged on the screen door. Dad peeked around the kitchen door at the far end of the dining room. He twirled his glass of lemonade to make the ice tinkle, took a long, exaggerated swig, and allowed as to how that was the best lemonade he'd ever tasted. "Absolutely deee-licious!"

Ocie yanked at the door a couple more times and then ran for the back door. It was locked also. He began to circle the house. My bedroom window was open. Just below the window was a little shed jetting out from the house. It held rakes, a push lawnmower, assorted gardening tools, and my Radio Flyer wagon. Ocie figured that if he could get on the roof of the shed, he could wriggle through the open window. The door to the shed was locked. He could not access anything to climb on. He jumped repeatedly but his fingers couldn't quite reach the sheds roof. He tried to shinny up the side of the shed by digging his fingers into the white shingles. Failing that, he talked me into getting down on all fours to form a step stool. Disappointingly, I collapsed. So, we continued to circle the house looking for a breach in the family fortress.

Ocie discovered a basement window ajar. He pushed. The hinge squeaked. He flattened himself across a nearly dormant lily-of-the-valley patch and peered inside. After a few moments, he squirmed and snaked himself through the window. I, of course, followed. We found ourselves sitting on the top of a mountain of coal. Ocie inched forward. A chunk gave way under his foot, and down he slid. I turned to escape back through the window, but the unstable coal gave way and I became part of the landslide that was over almost before it began. The two of us sat at the bottom of the coal heap, filthy dirty, perhaps a bit bruised, but essentially unharmed.

In the pale gray light of the basement, we cautiously negotiated our way past the monstrous coal furnace, the gaping black hole of the sump-pump, and the old Maytag washer with its nasty hand cranked wringer. Reaching the safety of the stairs that led to the kitchen, we tiptoed up the steps. The light from the basement windows became dimmer and dimmer. We knew we had reached the landing when we saw a thin ribbon of light creeping under the kitchen door. I started to giggle with relief. Ocie commanded me to shush.

It took him only a few seconds to locate the doorknob. He threw the door open and we rushed into the kitchen with shrill, wild, victorious screams. We had cornered our prey. Dad, obviously surprised, jumped up from his chair. He reached out, catching Ocie's towhead in the palm of his open hand as if it were a basketball. The next second I was also captured.

Dad had control of Ocie's head, but nothing was controlling his arms and legs. They twirled and kicked like a windup, tin plate toy gone berserk. "Hunka Ted's a big Bohemie," Ocie chanted. "Hunka Ted's a big Bohemie," I mimicked. Dad let out a deep guttural laugh. His eyes twinkled as he looked at Ocie. "You're a persistent little bugger, aren't you?" I didn't know what a "persistent little bugger" was, but from my Dad's amusement and the admiration in his voice as he held Ocie at bay, I knew I wanted to be one.

I'm not sure if this is a true childhood memory, or just a memory that has been created for me through the telling and retelling of the coal bin saga. I wonder, was the memory clip of the two of us bursting through the basement door into the kitchen etched in my mind's eye in 1938, or has it been created from hearing the story over and over at family gatherings? As a child, I doubt I would have been able to see everyone's personality as perfectly distilled as I see them today.

My memory has my mother standing at our bow-legged, cream and green Elmwood gas range. She didn't miss a beat as her wooden spoon gently stroked the sides of her double boiler. She shifted from her task just enough to observe the happenings about her. Taking everything in, but offering no comment, showing no sign of surprise, no utterance of approval or disapproval, she just watched life unfold around her with an air of detachment.

Dad immediately jumped up from his chair at the far end of our large white, drop-leaf kitchen table. He positioned himself to be in the center of the action. Without hesitation, he let out a war cry inviting us to challenge him and encouraging us to do our best, to try our hardest.

Ocie's father, who was at the near end of the table, leaned forward on the edge of his chair, his elbows on his knees and his head even with his son's. He provided strategy and encouraged his son to keep up the good fight. He coached, "That a boy, Oc. Go get him. Get low, son. Drop down, out of his reach, go for his ankles."

Ocie's ten -year-old sister, Thelma Leone, was in the living room reading a book on our itchy mohair sofa. She looked up just long enough to glance into the kitchen to view the ruckus. Satisfied that it was just her Uncle Ted, up to his usual antics, she returned to her book.

Ocie's mother was washing dishes at the wide, double drain-board porcelain sinks. She glanced over her shoulder. An eyebrow arched. She cocked her head, a clear signal to anyone who may have noticed that this bedlam was going to be short-lived. Although she was scarcely bigger than a minute, she twirled abruptly, took a definitive step into the fray, took Ocie Allen by the ear, and marched him off toward the bathroom. "Just look at the mess you've made of yourself young man." When it came to bringing order out of chaos, Ocie's mother was a woman of action.

As Ocie is marched from the room to undergo a spit and polish, the synergy and vibrancy of the action dissipates, and the memory fades.

Ruffian Warrior

My "wars of winter" began with the first significant snow-fall in 1943. The preparation for battle, however, began the month before my ninth birthday. Battles were raging in Europe. With the innocence of youth, and not fully understanding the realities of war, the kids of our neighborhood were excitedly anticipating the eruption of the snowball battles that would take place in the vacant lot catty-corner across the street from my backyard.

Each of us began to collect our war supplies. Imitating my father, I created a checklist of the materials I would need, and tacked it above my workbench, which was along the east wall of the basement, just to the left of my father's workbench. Next to my checklist, I posted several Crayola "blueprints" of the war equipment I was planning to collect or build.

The first thing on my list was my sled. I hauled it down from the attic, sanded and waxed the runners, greased the steering arm, and made sure the black rubber handgrips were tightly attached. I waxed and polished the shiny black wood with fancy red and gold designs. When standing upright, my sled was taller than I.

It was heavier than most sleds, with a complex blade and steering system. It could outdistance every other sled on the Riverside Park slope. The Junior Racers, Flexible Flyers, Radio Flyers, Flying Arrows, Fleeting Flashers, Speed-a-ways, Speedliners, Silver Streaks, Lightening Gliders, Yankee Clippers, Champions, and Comets could never match the distance of my Black Beauty. I took particular pride in the fact that the older boys would beg to borrow it for a ride or two, each boy trying to get closer to the banks of the Cedar River than the previous sledder.

Once my sled was shipshape I checked it off my supply list and moved on to the next item needed—two orange crates. For these I headed to Kadlec & James Grocery store. I was pretty sure Lester Kadlec would help me out, because every Saturday afternoon when Dad and I visited his grocery store, he gave me a sucker. I was right. He retrieved two wooden orange crates from his storeroom, and even helped me to secure them tightly across my Radio Flyer wagon. Mother allowed me to stack the orange crates on our enclosed back porch next to my dad's now-empty sauerkraut and pickle crocks.

Next on my list was extra-heavy cardboard. I checked all four grocery stores in the neighborhood. They had lots of cardboard boxes, but not a single extra-heavy one. My only option was to jump on my bike and head for Smulekoff's Furniture Store.

When going downtown, I always liked to take a shortcut across the railroad bridge at Penick & Ford, just because most other kids weren't allowed. The men in the switchyard knew me and let me pass because my uncle Fred was a switchman. I'd get off my bike and walk it through the switchyard, waving and smiling to the railroad men on duty. Every now and then a new man would come to shoo me away, but then another railway man would tell him I was okay, I was Fred's "snot-nosed niece" and knew the "rules of the rails." They knew I could be trusted to negotiate the wooden bridge planks that formed the walkway abutting the railroad tracks that crossed the Cedar River.

Even walking my bike across the bridge, the uneven planks made it a handful to control, especially when a plank or two was missing. I'd look down at the Cedar River rushing below me and wonder what would happen if I failed to jump across a gap, or stepped on a rotting plank that gave way. Would I fall through the gap? Would

I be carried away by the Cedar River and drown? That was worrisome, as I wasn't at all sure my behavior had been good enough to get me into heaven, and I sure didn't want to go to hell. It was all pretty scary.

One time I stopped and carefully measured the distance of one of the wider gaps. It was wider than my foot by quite a bit. I understood I must calculate my jumps very carefully. I always made it to the other side, except in an occasional nightmare. But even then, I always woke up before hitting the water.

At Smulekoff's I told the salesman I needed two large extra-heavy cardboard boxes delivered to my house. I asked the price and pulled out my coin purse. He said he didn't sell cardboard boxes, but sent me to make my request of a lady in the office. She was a bit surprised by my order and questioned my purpose. I explained I needed them for the coming winter's snowball wars. She smiled a knowing smile, took down my name, address, and telephone number. She said she would see what she could do. Within a few days two large cardboard appliance boxes were sitting on my front porch.

We kids all understood the importance of supply lines and the occasional necessity of a black market contact. Each of us prided ourselves that "we knew people, who knew people."

Paint was hard to come by. It wasn't rationed, but it was in short supply. Back then paint contained lead which was needed for the war effort. My friend, Mr. Matterson, played cards every week with an old man who had a stash of partly-used paint cans in his garage. He talked him into giving me a few nearly-empty cans. Once I removed the paint crust that formed on the surface, there was still an inch or so of paint that was perfectly good for painting my heavy cardboard. I had learned that cardboard painted with exterior paint was waterproof and could be used in a variety of ways.

Next on my list were extra-large tin cans. There was a lady who roomed across the street with the Stastny family. She worked in the kitchen of Mercy Hospital. Aunt Gwen suggested I ask her to get me some empty institutional-size tin cans. I did, and she did, but she made me promise to give them to the war effort come spring. To insure no one would know I was hording tin cans, I hid them in the corner of the coal bin, under a pile of coal.

I needed those tin cans because it was always necessary to haul additional snow into our war zone. Our battlefield never had enough snow to create our fortifications and provide sufficient ammunition. We would place a piece of cardboard across the seat of our sleds. On top of the cardboard, we would stand upright the institutional tin cans that were open on both ends. Then, we lassoed the collection of cans together with a clothesline. Once the cans were secured on the sled, our search and seize mission was quickly executed.

We shoveled snow into the cans, packed it down as hard as we could, and then hauled our snow-filled cylinders to our battlefield. There we pushed the packed snow bricks from their molds with a homemade ramrod, which was three can lids screwed together for strength and fastened to the end of a one-by-one piece of scrap of lumber.

Looking back, our building skills for the snow fort were quite sophisticated. We learned to level our footings, to taper our walls—making them wider at the bottom than at the top—and to offset our building blocks for strength. The older kids taught the younger ones.

The center of the vacant lot was considered a no-man's land. It was bordered east and west by a two-foot high defensive snow wall that we kids built. Six feet

behind that first wall we built a second snow wall. A few yards further along was the fort itself, a large circle about six feet in diameter with three-foot walls that had crenellations every few feet to provide a clear view of the approaches.

When I became an officer, I attempted to innovate. I constructed cardboard shields, which I controlled with a system of armbands and grips. The first attempts didn't last the season. I had glued the cardboard together using Elmer's Glue-All. It wasn't waterproof, and the shields fell apart after only one damp snowball battle.

My second innovation was a humongous body shield that left no body part exposed to enemy snowballs. I made sure this one didn't fall apart. I waterproofed the cardboard with house paint, then stitched it together with carpet thread. I covered the edges with duct tape, so damp snow couldn't sneak in. I also used steel washers to reinforce the heavy rope armbands and grips. My body shield was designed to last the duration. It proved to be a magnificent defense against flying snowballs. However, it was too bulky for conducting an aggressive offense. After using it in battle for only one day, I cut it down to protect only my head and shoulders.

After watching us at battle one afternoon, Joe Blom, known in the neighborhood as "Bachelor Blom," coached me to build a catapult. Within a week, both sides were experimenting with that new technology. Our first catapults were stationary and cumbersome. Listening to my complaints, Harry Farmer suggested I fasten the fulcrum of the catapult to my sled to make a mobile unit. That worked better, but still wasn't as fast or as satisfying as a running advance, which allowed us to deliver snow grenades more quickly and with greater accuracy. The catapults were soon abandoned on the field of battle.

My only innovation that lasted, was created in my first year as a ruffian warrior, while I was still a lowly private. It was my mobile ammunition carrier. I had tied an orange crate to my sled, filled it with snowballs, and followed the infantry into battle. I received a nice battlefield promotion for that innovation. Even as kids we understood the hierarchy of command, and we knew that good ideas and experience could trump age. The commanding officer allowed me to lead troops into battle; although, if the truth be told, sometimes the platoon that agreed to follow me consisted solely of my faithful beagle-hound Tippy.

I have no idea how many generations of ruffian warriors fought their wars of winter on that vacant lot across from my K Street house. In writing this remembrance, I find it chilling to realize that the generals who taught me to build with snow, were serving in the United States Armed Services by the time I became a snow fort general. Some of them never returned from those foreign battlefields to dry their mittens on a rack near the radiator, or sit at the kitchen table to sip a mug of hot cocoa and dunk their freshly-baked oatmeal-raisin cookies.

The Kayak

Sandra knew she best stay out of the way. She huddled between the cupboard and the kitchen table trying to make herself as small as possible. Through the basement doorway, she watched the red tip of the kayak that her father had built over the winter, bobble up and down, and back and forth.

"Won't make it," Sandra's Uncle Fred growled. In her imagination she could see the stub of his unlit cigar bobbing between his tobacco-stained teeth.

"Dammit, I can see that! Don't need you tellin' me." Sandra's father snapped at his older brother.

"Can't hold this baby here all day."

"Okay, okay, okay, ease her back down the stairs." Sandra could hear the frustration and disappointment in her dad's voice.

As the tip of the kayak receded from sight, she tiptoed to the head of the stairs, got down on her tummy, and peered around the door jamb. Slowly the two men continued to make their way back down the basement stairs. When they were clear, Sandra settled herself on the fourth step from the top, where she could see everything, but remain out of the way.

Uncle Fred sat on a nail keg, eyeing Sandra's father, "Well Ted, wha'da'ya gonna tell everybody?"

"Nothin."

"Don't think that's an option. You have little miss blabber-mouth sitting right up there on the stairs. The whole neighborhood will know by noon."

"Will not!" Sandra protested. "I won't tell nobody." And she didn't. The kayak, covered with a tarp, rested on the sawhorses the remainder of April, then May, June, and most of July.

Every now and then, Sandra's Aunt Gwen would complain about the kayak being in her way when she did the laundry. Ted would promise to 'get-around-to-it', but he never managed to. Instead, the household, and the neighborhood, settled into their summer routines.

In the evenings, Sandra's front porch was the gathering place for all ages. Her friends came to play catch, tag, kick-the-can, or hide-n-seek. The teenage boys in the neighborhood came to gossip and exchange small talk with her father and flirt with the girls, who came to flirt with the boys. The adult neighbors just came to gossip, worry about the war, and complain about rationing.

One evening, with the high school boys gathered around Ted, he queried no one in particular, "How's your summer training coming along?"

"What'da'ya mean?" Harry Farmer asked.

"You boys trainin' everyday so you'll be in shape for football when school starts?"

"Coach won't be starting training for another month," Tommy Gains responded.

"You aren't workin' out on your own?"

"Doin' what?" Frank Stasney asked.

Ted let that float on the air for a little more than a minute. "Instead of wasting your afternoons horsing around, perhaps you should do something to build up your muscles."

"Like Frank said, doin' what?" Harry asked.

"Get a farm job loading bales, or maybe digging ditches on a road gang. Any job that gets those muscles working. No pain, no gain. Isn't that what your coach says?" The boys nodded. The subject changed.

The next night, and the night after that, and every night for the rest of the week, Sandra's dad asked, "How's your training coming?" When Friday night rolled around he said, "Still not training? Okay, I'm gonna take mercy on you guys. You show up here tomorrow morning at seven sharp. I'll have a couple of pick axes and some shovels. You can bring any of your teammates that you think will benefit from some good muscle-building hard work. Show me you know how to work, and I may let you help me dig a fruit cellar."

Four guys showed up Saturday, six on Sunday. The following Saturday there were more kids than shovels. They argued about who had the right to work. Ted got out his stop watch, and set up relay teams to compete against one another. The girls sat on the mounds of dirt cheering their guys on. Sandra was appointed as the fetch-it-girl. She ran for water, Coke, and Orange Crush pop; Hersey and Baby Ruth candy bars; work gloves and Band-Aids.

Sandra and her playmate, Steven Ammons, also started a tally sheet to count the number of wheelbarrows of dirt hauled to a dump truck her father had borrowed. They made themselves unofficially responsible for a tool inventory.

It took several days to dig the eight-foot x eight-foot x eight-foot hole, but when they had finished, the stone rubble wall of the basement was exposed. The next step was to knock a hole through that wall to provide access into the basement. For that job, only one guy at a time was allowed to wield a pick ax. Since they all wanted the job, Ted suggested twenty strokes per man. Everyone else stood on the sidelines yelling out the strokes: one, two, three, four, …. Before the day was out, they had opened the wall, and Ted had instructed them in framing a doorway.

The next weekend the relay teams were back. They competed to see which team would be the first to get their molds in place for pouring the concrete footings. There was no holding them back. Ted demonstrated how to mix concrete, and the footings were poured. Little Miss Fetch-it was kept very busy making and serving Kool-Aid and popcorn.

The footings cured for a week. The next Saturday Ted demonstrated how use a plumb line, and layup concrete blocks. The next day, the boys would have their turn to layup concrete blocks.

There were a lot of kids who missed church that Sunday. Two teams began just after breakfast to lay up the blocks. It was near four in the afternoon when the job was finished. Sandra's father stood in the new doorway, between the dark basement and the sun-drenched hole that was slowly becoming the new fruit cellar.

"Nice job, men. These walls will have to cure. We'll put the roof on next weekend. Let's celebrate our progress. Who would like to join me at Riverside Park to christen the kayak I built last winter?"

Everyone cheered. The boys hoisted the kayak off the sawhorses, carried it through the doorway they had made, and gently lifted it up into the back yard. Then with four guys on each side of the kayak, they jogged the block to Riverside Park. Sandra inserted herself between a couple of the guys and ran right along with them. A fireman spotted them coming and called to the other men on duty. They clustered on the hill near the firehouse to watch the procession make its way to the west bank of the Cedar River.

Fireman Tony Ipsen, who always took a short cut through Sandra's yard on his way to and from his duties at the fire station, called out good naturedly, "You guys gonna take a chance on that Bohemi-built kayak? Hope you all know how to swim."

The kids laughed. Everyone was in high spirits as both groups bantered back and forth good naturedly. "We'll get our rescue equipment ready," one of the firemen teased.

Instead of Champagne, the kayak was launched with a bottle of Orange Crush. The youthful athletes paddled the kayak with ease and precision. Ted, on the other hand, could not stay upright. Again and again, after only a few strokes, the kayak flipped over, tossing him into the Cedar River. The audience on the river bank cheered and catcalled wildly each time.

The chief and a couple of firemen sauntered down carrying four life-saver rings and suggested, "You boys might want to jump in and rescue Ted."

"For real?" Harry Farmer asked, knowing you weren't supposed to swim in the Cedar River at Riverside Park.

The chief nodded, "It's a rescue mission, but only four guys at a time."

After the first of many rescue missions that would occur that afternoon, Ted retrieved four buckets from behind a bush. Each had a long rope fastened to its handle. He threw a bucket into the river, hauled it ashore, and poured the water over Sandra's head. She screamed with surprise and joy. He handed her a bucket. Following her father's example, she threw it into the river, hauled it ashore, and doused Dorothy Matterson. The water fights were on. Even the girls, who were not part of a rescue mission, enjoyed the river that afternoon.

A short time later, Aunt Gwen showed up pulling Sandra's Radio Flyer which was filled with a picnic of egg salad sandwiches, potato chips, and lemonade for everyone, including the firemen.

What ten-year-old Sandra was too young to see, is crystal clear to eighty-three-year-old Sandra. As a child she admired her father's cleverness in getting his kayak out of the basement. Today, she can appreciate his rare skill as a master community builder.

Helga C. W. Mayhew

"With confidence and a positive attitude, almost everything can be turned into a small or big adventure." Helga admits to a wanderlust that has taken her to various countries in Europe, Central and South America, Africa, and the Middle East.

Helga was born in West Prussia, now Poland. During World War II her family fled across the Baltic Sea to Denmark to escape the advancing Russian Army. After two years in a refugee camp, her family was allowed to move to West Germany. Helga graduated from a technical college in Berlin, and worked five years in West Germany. She then immigrated to the United States, where she raised her family. Helga has had a successful career as both an electronics design engineer and an environmental engineer. Read on to enjoy some of her adventures.

Adventures of a
Wooden Suitcase

I don't know exactly where the tree grew or was felled that provided the material for my being. I was put together and painted brown in a refugee camp in Denmark by a German refugee carpenter in 1947. I am a very simple suitcase with a handle and a hasp, 25 inches long, 16.5 inches wide, and 8.5 inches deep, with a pretty interesting history. I am nothing like those much fancier suitcases, that can report about great trips into exotic countries and beautiful parks around the world.

I became a precious gift to a German mother and her four children in 1947. They had arrived in this camp in May 1945 after crossing the Baltic Sea from West Prussia as the Russian armies were closing in on them at the end of World War II. The family had arrived on Danish soil with a few belongings, mostly clothes for the children and a small wicker basket where the six-month old baby was sleeping. In the straw mattress the mother had hidden her jewelry, important papers, and some small valuables which she later used to pay for medicine for her children.

Over the more than two years in this camp, the family had acquired some new clothing and some household goods like towels and spoons. When it was finally time for the family to repatriate to West Germany, the mother had nothing into which to pack her few possessions. That's where and why she received me, the wooden brown suitcase. Over the next four years I participated in at least six different moves as the family was relocated from one camp to another and to various apartments in West Germany. I was sturdy and strong, safely keeping fragile and important items. After the last move to their own house in 1951, I was stored in the back of a deep closet and almost forgotten.

Then one day in 1967, the eldest daughter of the family, Helga, had returned all the way from America to be married in the church in which she had been baptized about twelve years earlier at the age of fifteen. She received many presents and was in need of an extra sturdy container to take the gifts and her trousseau with her on her long voyage back to the USA. Her father remembered ME just waiting for another adventure. I was dusted off, lined with some plastic bubbles and towels, and prepared for a new journey.

For the return honeymoon trip the newlyweds had booked passage on the transatlantic liner, the SS France. We travelled by train to Paris, and after a few days for the couple to explore the city, we took the train to the harbor of Le Havre at the English Channel. We three boarded the ship and after a short stop at Southampton, England, we began the crossing of the Atlantic Ocean to New York. The couple slept in a cozy cabin while I kept company with all the other pieces of luggage in the cargo hold.

During the passage we encountered some rough seas, and I heard that the young woman did not feel so well. However, being honored on her 28th birthday with a reception, and then being invited to sit at the captain's table for dinner, must have made up for it. In New York we left the ship after inspection and we three took another train ride to Fort Wayne, Indiana. From there it was only a short ride to Hicksville, Ohio. A year later, in August 1968, we moved from the small town to Columbus, Ohio, where the husband attended the university and the wife worked in the University Electro-Science Laboratory.

After five years, in 1973, I was filled up again with goods and travelled in a moving truck to Cedar Rapids, Iowa. After two more moves within the city, I was un-packed and stored again in the back of a closet, where I rested for the next forty-two years. I was discovered by the children of the honeymoon couple as they were cleaning out the house after their father's death. I am now sitting on Helga's porch where I am supporting a big vase with flowers.

Visitors notice my colorful sticker SS France, which I am proudly displaying, and which brings with it many, many memories of more than seven decades. Now I am wondering what might happen next.

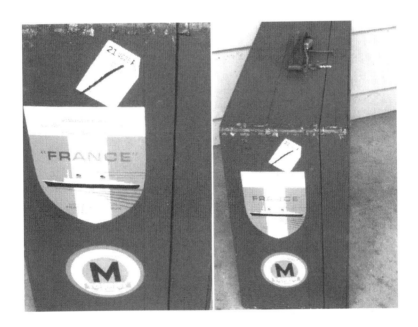

Helga C. W. Mayhew

November Memories

The biggest event in my life was calculated to happen at the end of December 1974. Therefore, I was very much looking forward to the arrival of my mother who was to share with me the time of expectation. We were to go shopping together for anything that might be needed to welcome my baby into this world.

Well, nature decided differently. To everyone's surprise, my twin boys were born on a Monday in November. My mother was supposed to arrive on the following Friday. The babies weighed four pounds eight ounces and four pounds fifteen ounces. They had to spend their next ten days in their incubators until they reached at least five pounds.

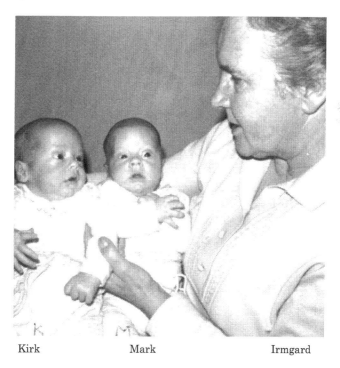

Kirk   Mark   Irmgard

103

The usual hospital stay for mothers at that time was five days, but since the babies were well cared for, the doctor gave me permission to leave a day early, so we could pick up my mother from the airport. I did not inform my family in Germany about the surprise, until I knew my mother was safely on her way, since I was worried that in the excitement she would get confused during her first trip to Iowa. My husband insisted on carting me in a wheelchair around the airport. This almost gave my mother a heart attack, thinking that I had lost the baby. Oh no! I showed her the wristbands marked "Baby A" and "Baby B" to assure her that all was well.

Besides several trips to the hospital every day to feed and cuddle the babies, we were busy visiting many mothers of twins, members of the Mothers of Twins Club, where we found most everything we needed in duplicate, from clothes to cribs. Once we brought our babies home, it was around-the-clock feeding, diapering, and cuddling. During these times, both of us sitting comfortable and warm, my mother's memories of days exactly thirty years earlier came flooding back to her in vivid colors, when she held my baby brother in her arms. The following are her recollections of the worries and fears of those days so long ago, as best as I can remember them.

The war had started on September 1, 1939, but in the Fall of 1944 we still lived on our farm in West Prussia, Germany. My father was stationed in Austria and my pregnant mother was responsible for eight families living and working on our farm, consisting of thirty-eight persons. It included her three children, her parents-in-law, and several servants.

The news from the Eastern Front was terrifying. Wave upon wave of refugees were passing nearby, slowing down traffic to a crawl on all roads leading west, fleeing from the advancing Russian Army. For many weeks, day and night, the noises of squeaking wheels, neighing horses, howling dogs, crying babies, and lamenting voices traveled the distance to the farmhouse.

Everything was prepared and packed into two coaches and seven wagons, while our group waited for permission from the county officials to join the throng at the tail end. If people left earlier and got caught with a Personalausweis (Personal Identification Card) from their home county not yet cleared for evacuation, they might get shot by patrolling soldiers.

In November, the fourth child was born, my brother Hartmut. And still no permission to leave. Every so often, some groups stopped by the farm asking for food and shelter, reporting gruesome stories. Some help was given where possible and the groups moved on. Our family and the seven farmhands, with their families, had to wait until the 26th of January 1945, when official permission was granted that all citizens of the county of Grosses Werder (Great Werder County) were allowed to leave. It was my mother's 28th birthday. In our horse-drawn coach, a wicker basket, filled with straw and blankets, served as baby Hartmut's carrier. Underneath it all, my mother hid her jewelry, important documents, and cash, which later became very important.

During these weeks of waiting, the German forces were in retreat towards the west, while the Russian troops had moved south of Prussia towards the west and then north, controlling bridges across the river Vistula, entrapping people and soldiers. In addition, the German army blocked the civilian population from using primary roads that were reserved for German troops. To the north the Baltic Sea stopped the escape by land. News had slowly spread through the population that Russian submarines were patrolling the sea. On January 30th, 1945 the German cruise ship MV Wilhelm Gustloff, turned military transport and then refugee carrier, was attacked. An estimated 9,400 souls were sent to their icy deaths.

It was one of the coldest winters in people's memory, and many perished, as did many farm animals which had been set free. Being blocked by the Russian army from moving to the west, my mother and her dwindling group moved in circles always following rumors where there may be an opening to the west. One by one the other families had been separated from the group, and at last, only her in-laws, the children's nanny, and the coachman were supporting her.

In April they finally turned toward the Baltic Sea, where ships were leaving from various points along the coast to Denmark and Sweden. Many of the people who did not get a chance to leave from these coastal camps were later captured by the Russian army, killed, or transported to Siberia. My grandparents were admitted to one of the camps in Germany, and eventually landed in a refugee camp in Denmark. There, my grandmother passed away, succumbing to breast cancer.

Many incidents occurred during that harrowing time on the road that seemed to hint at the presence of a protecting angel. At least that is how my mother felt at that time, and still believed until she passed away. One time, the coachman had hidden the coach under a tree and moved the family into a deserted house. My mother left the house to find a cow to milk when a low-flying fighter strafed the house. When my mother hurried back fearing the worst, she heard crying from a chicken coop, where our nanny had taken us when she heard the approaching airplane. All were safe.

By that time, my older brother, my sister, and I had contracted measles. Therefore, the camp officials turned my mother and her charges away, fearing that the people in the camp might get infected. My baby brother was severely undernourished, had typhus, and was covered with sores. A passing German military doctor handed my mother his rations and salves to treat the inflammations. Traveling in the wicker basket, with no way to keep him clean and dry most of the time, he had no more strength for crying. So the doctor hinted that my mother should abandon him to save her strength for the other three children.

After spending additional time in either abandoned houses or in holes in the dike, my mother finally secured a crossing for us from Gotenhafen, now Gdynia, Poland on a small military ship loaded with severely wounded soldiers. The officer told her, "Come on board, many of these soldiers will most likely not survive the passage; measles will not hurt them." The nanny and the coachman helped loading our belongings and then drove off with the coach. We learned much later that they returned to their village in Poland, got married, and named their first son Hartmut, after my little brother.

On May 2nd, we safely reached the shores of Denmark and were allowed to land, since the German army still occupied Denmark until May 5th. As she was leaving the boat, a German officer handed my mother his last money, since he expected to be captured as the war was coming to an end. She later recalled that after that most fearful hundred-day journey, this was the moment when she realized that she was now a person without a home and a country. She was faced with an unknown future for her and her children.

Eventually, we were assigned to the refugee Camp Rye, living in army barracks. We stayed for more than two years, since the Danish government was ordered by the three victorious military authorities (America, England, and France) to keep the refugees until housing could be found in the western occupied zones. After the end of the war, the three Allies were overwhelmed to locate housing for the refugees who had safely arrived in the three western zones. Many refugees who had landed in various other countries also had to wait for repatriation to West Germany, as the three zones were later named.

All the children were sick, each cared for in a different outside hospital. My mother got permission to leave the camp to visit us. Selling her jewelry and her money on the black market, she could buy some needed medicine for us. Only my baby brother, Hartmut, did not respond to any treatment, until as a last resort, the lady doctor suggested that my mother donate blood. After three transfusions of her blood, Hartmut finally began to thrive, and after three months could finally join us. My mother did not realize how lucky we had been. In 2005, five years after her death, her children learned "that the Danish Association of Doctors had decided in March 1945 that German refugees would not receive any medical care. The Red Cross agreed, and as a result, about 80% of the small children that landed on Denmark's shores did not survive the following months. Nutrition was terrible in all camps, in total 13,000 people died in 1945 alone, of them 7,000 children."[1]

---

[1] Translated by Helga Mayhew from *Spiegel Online*, 5/16/2005.

Turning six years old in the camp, I received some schooling organized by a refugee council. With no writing material or books, we had to memorize everything. This served me very well, when I later attended regular schools in West Germany. The camp council set up a variety of committees to pool resources and to keep people occupied with many different activities. I remember that my mother taught us songs and dances and wrote little plays for the children to perform.

Dieter   Irmgard   Hartmut   Heinz   Helga Heidrun

My mother's mother, who had arrived in western Germany shortly before the war ended, finally secured housing for us in Low Saxony. We arrived back in western Germany in Spring 1948. We were assigned to a farming family who cleared out two rooms for us. There, my father joined us in Fall 1948, having been released from an American prisoner of war camp. In 1949, the Blyle Clothing Company donated one piece of new clothing for each of us. I received a bright red dress, my favorite color to this day. This was a reason to take a picture of our united family. A new beginning promised a better future for all.

Hartmut   Heidrun   Helga   Dieter

Helga C. W. Mayhew

Kingdom in the Sky: Crossing Lesotho

My brother Dieter and I headed from Bethlehem, Free State, South Africa towards Durban on the Indian Ocean. Between us and our destination were the Drakensberge, a range of high mountains forming the border between the southeast area of South Africa, the province of Kwa-Zulu-Natal, and the small kingdom of Lesotho. We had the option to drive around the mountain range or cross through Lesotho, the "Kingdom in the Sky." "Drakensberge" means "Dragon Mountains" in Dutch. The Zulu people call it "Barrier of upward-pointing Spears," an accurate description of the sheer and jagged ridges of the most spectacular section of the mountain range.

Lesotho is located on a high plateau in the middle of South Africa. My brother had always had this special dream to cross through Lesotho. He told me that this road, the world-famous Sani Pass, is a very treacherous mountain road maintained by 4x4 clubs for special races. It would be a challenging ride; did I want to do it. "As long as you are doing the driving, I am game!" And what a ride it was! During the first half of the trip, the uphill paved road was peppered with deep holes; Dieter often had to decide in an instant which hole was the least dangerous to drive through. Fortunately, oncoming traffic was almost non-existent, therefore weaving from one side to the other was possible. Halfway up the drive we met a road crew of five or six people who were filling in the holes with fresh asphalt, but further up, people had driven over the fresh asphalt and partly opened up the holes again. Job security?

After a short stop at the City of Mokhotlong we crossed over the Mahlaselo Pass at 3,222 meters or about 10,571 feet, and passed near the top of the Drakensberg, the mountain Thabana-Ntlenyana, the highest peak in all of South Africa at 3,482 meters or about 11,424 feet. We arrived at the southern Lesotho border checkpoint in the afternoon and noticed "the highest pub" in South Africa across from the guard house. The border consisted of barbed wire stretched between some simple fence posts. All was very casual, a quick stamp into our passports and we were on our way downhill!

Leaving the Lesotho guard post we started the roller-coaster ride down into KwaZulu-Natal. The dirt road was washed out with deep ruts at many places. Big boulders had rolled onto the track. To avoid them, our truck had to swerve from side to side, bringing us close to the abyss! The truck hopped and careened, and I held on for dear life! While my brother was maneuvering around the steep curves, I was looking out for oncoming traffic. The rule of the road is that whoever comes up has the right-of-way. Twice we had to get off the track to let trucks pass laboring up the steep mountain.

We stopped at a few points to collect rocks, take pictures, and just enjoy the scenery, and a little time to relax. We couldn't linger long since behind us clouds were rolling down the mountain sides. Darker clouds were gathering as we entered a steep canyon, almost chasing us with thunder and lightning. We were looking forward to a more relaxed ride at the foot of the mountain and to rest in the next larger town.

Suddenly, around the bend, we came to a screeching halt in front of a rickety closed gate! Really, it was just

some metal tubing with wires strung across. Our truck could have easily crashed right through it!

Further down we could see an official-looking building. My brother went to ask permission to pass the gate. "Sorry, South Africa closes at 4:00 PM!"

"Can't you please let us through? We are only 15 minutes late and a storm is approaching".

"Cannot do that, the State would have to pay me overtime! Go and talk to my boss in the house on top of the hill".

By the time Dieter returned, shaking his head, thunder and lightning were overhead. I suggested offering the guard that we would gladly pay the overtime. Oh no, that could be interpreted as a bribe and we could disappear for a while! A little power play! We had no cell phone to contact anyone to let them know about our predicament. Beyond the building there was another rickety gate, where a young man and two young women in a truck were pleading to be allowed to ride up the pass. No such luck either!

A crack and thunder prompted my brother to quickly climb into the cab, before a deluge shook the truck. A little earlier we had crossed a trickle of a stream, which in no time turned into a roaring river. Dieter hurried to back the truck further up to a flat space, where we waited out the storm. I found this whole situation so funny, I could not stop from laughing.

"South Africa closes at 4 PM!?!"

That made Dieter even more furious remembering a similar episode. A few years before, when he had been traveling with his wife, they had crossed through Swaziland to enter Krueger Park from the south. As they arrived at the border into South Africa shortly after 5:00 PM, "Sorry, the border closes at 5:00 PM". His wife never forgave him for not knowing about country closing times.

And now it had happened again! Oh, was my brother mad at himself!

Forget about setting up a tent or cooking tonight! When the rain slowed down, we packed as much as possible into the cab, each got an apple, and I had to share my tight quarters in the truck bed with my brother! During this trip, my brother usually slept in a one-man tent while I enjoyed the luxury of a mattress in the truck.

The next morning, not too well rested, we crawled out of the truck. After some good bends and stretches in the cool air, we gratefully looked at a cloudless sky. All was wet, and setting up for breakfast was not possible.

The cold water rushing down from the mountains was clear and refreshing, and splashing our faces with it lifted our spirits. There was plenty of water for coffee and tea. We were ready for a new day. On the dot, the gates opened at 8:00 AM, we got our passports stamped, and off we went forward to more adventures.

Ed Popelka

Ed is an adventurer. In his childhood story "Rescuing Ricky" he finds adventure in his own back yard.

In Junior High, Ed falls in love—not with a gorgeous girl, but with the mobility and speed of his "Whizzer." From this point on, Ed continues "Gaining Momentum."

After graduating from the University of Iowa with a degree in Economics, he seeks adventure in California's large cities, mountains, deserts, ocean beaches, and film scene. As a salesman for Itek Business Supplies Ed finds fertile ground to advance his career and to pursue an adventurous lifestyle. He finds opportunities to rev the engines of several Montesa Motorcycles, a Mercedes 280SL automobile, and a Bonanza airplane.

Today, life has come full circle for Ed. He has returned to Iowa and a career in real estate. He continues to find adventure—occasionally in his own backyard.

116

Rescuing Ricky

The Popelka family story-and-a-half Craftsman bungalow was built from 1932 to 1934 by Eddie's dad,
grampa, uncle, and assorted friends and workmen. At
that time, they did not have city water or sewer, but
they did have a good well for cooking and drinking water. They also had a large hand-dug and brick-lined cistern to catch rain water that was used for washing
clothes and other needs. They had installed a septic
system, and an inside toilet in their new home, but left
the outhouse in place.

Those of you who have had the experience of using
an "outdoor biffy," know it was many times quicker and
more convenient to use that facility rather than interrupt
a good game of tag, or whatever else was in process when
nature called.

In 1948, Ricky, a cocker spaniel, and five-year old Eddie, were pretty much inseparable buddies, at least during the day. Wherever Eddie went, Ricky was sure to go.
This particular beautiful, warm, sunny summer day was
no different in most respects. Unfortunately, there was
one almost disastrous difference on this particular day.
Little Eddie opened the door and popped into the biffy,
holding the door open for Ricky to come in too, which he
always did. After getting settled in, Ricky decided that
rather than continuing to sit on the floor of the biffy, he
would jump up and sit next to his best friend, Eddie. Perhaps, most of you can quickly envision what actually happened on that beautiful summer day.

Yes, those of you who pictured Ricky plunging into
the "muck" quite a ways below, due to this being a "two-
holer," are right. You would also be right if you said to
yourself, there is no way that kid is going to watch his

best buddy die in that biffy. There was zero hesitation. The rescue began immediately.

Since the moniker, "Little Eddie," fit this five-year-old quite well, he was small enough to slip through the hole. He was also very much like a squirrel when it came to climbing up and down trees, fences, and walls. Anything that presented a bit of a challenge, this kid was sure to test his ability to master. Quite fortunately, Eddie was able to figure out a way to lower himself down far enough, still hanging on to various parts of the biffy, to reach down with one hand and scoop up Ricky, hoist him up to his belly, while the dog continued to drip and shed muck all over every body-part of Eddie. He then had to figure out how-on-earth to lift the dog higher, and push him up through one of the two holes above his head.

It could correctly be described as amazing that both Ricky and Eddie emerged from that biffy, albeit a lot worse for wear. Upon exiting the biffy, Eddie called rather loudly for his mom, who quickly responded, being able to ascertain that she was urgently needed by her son. Can you even imagine the look on her face when she saw her son with his (and her) favorite dog? As moms always do, she rose to the occasion by filling a wash tub full of hot soapy water, disrobing her son in front of God, neighbor kids and all, outside in the yard, and cleaned them both thoroughly. Man, are kids and dogs really worth all the work and heartache they require?

Ed Popelka

Whizzing Along

My first manifestation of a passionate love was with motorcycles. I, like many young people, did not know the meaning of fear or risk. Climbing tall trees could be risky? I sure never thought so. I was not yet old enough, or more appropriately, had not been injured in a truly life-threating way, to avoid high level, high risk situations. But I digress.

This story is about my uncle Harry and the Whizzer motorbike he rebuilt for me. Uncle Harry was a genuine character. He and I really got along well. What a great buddy he was.

He lived in a small bungalow with a two-car garage behind. That garage was really something. There was just enough room for him to squeeze his car into the garage; the rest was jam packed with drill presses, lathes, benches, vices, and other tools. Here is where I loved to watch him do so many amazing things.

Uncle Harry was a mechanical genius-inventor. It was in this shop that he took a bedraggled Whizzer motorbike and rebuilt it from the ground up just for me.

The year was 1954. I was a twelve-year-old seventh grader at Roosevelt Junior High School. Needless to say, I was pretty excited about getting this motorbike. However, it didn't happen right away, since my uncle had a fulltime job at Collins Radio as a tool and die maker. It took him a number of weeks to complete all the work to make the Whizzer look and run well, and be safe for a kid to ride.

Of course, I wanted Uncle Harry to get it finished quickly, but there was no rushing him. He did not take shortcuts or do the job in a haphazard way. As a young kid that was a great way to learn the lesson; if you are going to do a job, you have to put in the time and effort to do it right. Cutting corners and rushing were not allowed, at least not in Uncle Harry's domain.

Eventually the day did come when the Whizzer was ready for me to take on a trial run. It ran like a top after it had gone through Uncle Harry's shop, and looked real sharp too. It was a reddish-brown color, with cream-colored striping, and a nice big comfortable saddle seat.

The motor fit above the pedals. Yes, it actually did have pedals. You would start out pedaling, and once you were moving you would start the motor. Once the motor started, you could go pretty fast, a lot faster than I could pedal a bicycle, even on a flat street. That motor could generate about 2.5 horsepower, and propel the bike up to about 40 mph on a flat road.

The gas tank was above the motor and held about three-fourths of a gallon of gas. I could go a long way with that amount. My Whizzer probably got about fifty miles to the gallon, so I did not have to fill it up very often. Dad always had a five-gallon can of gas in our garage, so it was easy for me to fill it up when it needed more gas.

I admit when it came to dependability my Whizzer motorbike was somewhat temperamental, but that didn't bother me one bit. I enjoyed the challenge. I rode it a lot in warm weather, and I did ride it to school. My friends were really impressed.

After a couple of years I found riding at 35-45 mph began to feel rather slow. I had older friends, including my brother, who rode real motorcycles. I wanted to experience, on my own, the speed and exhilaration I felt when I rode on the back of their cycles.

I'll always have fond memories of my Whizzer. It definitely stroked my passion for motorcycles.

Ed Popelka

The 200cc Triumph Cub

I lobbied my parents relentlessly for a superfast 500cc motorcycle, to no avail. My parents had been advised by our family doctor that a motorcycle was simply an accident on its way to happen. But I believed my life would soon come to end if I did not have a motorcycle.

Then, in the fall of 1957 I had an opportunity to buy a pretty tame 200cc Triumph Cub from an older student who attended Jefferson High School. I actually got my father to take me to this guy's home to see it. Like my Uncle Harry, my father very much appreciated good workmanship. He was favorably impressed with the looks and the quality of the machine. The fellow was asking $150, which was a good chunk of money, yet an affordable amount. I was totally excited and delighted when my Dad agreed to buy it for me. We set up a time to complete the transaction. On the appointed day we went to pay and take possession.

That was the day my passion, or as some might say my affliction, known as motorcycle mania, was shattered by the gods. The teenage owner of that fantastic 200cc Triumph Cub motorcycle reneged on selling it to me. It was the one that got away. My quest to possess had absolutely failed. As you might well imagine, I was an utterly disappointed kid, at least for several miserable days.

The TR 6

My passion for, or as some might say, my affliction, known as *motorcycle mania,* was shattered by the gods when a teenage owner of a fantastic 200cc Triumph Cub motorcycle reneged on selling it to me. As you might well imagine, I was an utterly disappointed kid, at least for several miserable days.

Now, let's fast forward. It was the summer of 1963. I had re-enrolled at the U of I for the fall semester. Along with two other guys, one from Marion and one from Chicago, I rented a house in Iowa City, just south of Highway 6, near Proctor & Gamble. We made quite the threesome. I was majoring in economics, our roommate from Marion was majoring in geology, and our Chicago guy, "Mr. Brainiac," was on his way to becoming an actuary, which most of you may remember, is a highfalutin mathematician that tells life insurance companies what they need to charge for premiums, to stay in business.

What you may ask, does all this have to do with a motorcycle maniac? To which I must respond, "Patience: Is it not important as a writer, to set the stage properly, so that you may better envision the story as it unfolds? However, on the other hand, perhaps I take too much liberty, as a writer of my memoirs. I shall leave you each to judge me, as you will."

Five long years have elapsed since the loss of the 200cc Triumph Cub. But, hark! During the fall of 1963, my parents had taken a trip to southern California to see my brother Ron and his family. For some reason, I decided to visit Pazour Motorcycles on "The Avenue" in Czech Village in Cedar Rapids. It was there that I saw and rode the big brother to the smaller Triumph Cub. It was a TR6, a full-sized 650cc twin-cylinder bike. To my delight, it was priced at $175. It needed some mechanical and cosmetic work. I ended up having the work done, including a green and white tucked and rolled new upholstery job on the seat. Man, what a beauty! With my parents in California, and me reaching the ripe old age of twenty-one in September, I made the decision to purchase it without first getting parental approval. Hallelujah!!

Forward Ho! There were a number of Indian Summer days that fall which filled me with pure joy, as I rode my TR6 west on Highway 6 in Iowa City. The bike ran perfectly, even as I would run it up to 90 to 100 miles per hour for brief periods. Sun shining, warm weather, my trusted steed and I, simply experiencing nature at its best.

In order for the reader to have a well-developed picture of the unfolding of various events that make up this, far from complete story of my life, I must provide some fleshing out of things that have no connection to motorcycles at all.

Once I was admitted to the U of I College of Business I was invited to become a member of Alpha Kappa Psi Business Fraternity. The AKP did not have a physical house on campus. We were quite active in many programs that further advanced our business education in a number of ways. We fraternity brothers also became very good friends and spent a fair amount of time doing social things in addition to business education matters.

The story I am about to tell, includes an AKP brother John, the grand and glorious TR6, and a little outing with the two of us jumping on my bike and taking a rather short ride over the streets of Iowa City, to one of our favorite "watering holes." We had a beer or two, no more, and re-boarded the revered Triumph to take John to his home in Iowa City. He, of course, sat on the seat behind me. The TR6 was designed and equipped to carry two people comfortably.

For those of you who are familiar with Iowa City, per my recollection, the bar we had chosen was on South Clinton Street, just south of the railroad tracks. Our route back to John's apartment took us north on Clinton. Because the track crossing was pretty rough to drive over (remember this was 1963, when railroad crossings were anything but smooth) I had slowed the bike to perhaps 5mph as I crossed the tracks.

WHAM!!! Without any warning, a pick-up truck SLAMMED into the back of the bike. Both John and I were thrown to the street. The TR6 sustained major damage. John and I remained conscious, as a number of people including the police gathered around us. I was able to get up and move about. It appeared that I had not sustained serious injuries. However, John was propelled into the front of the truck as it hit the back of the motorcycle. He was in significant pain. His back had taken the brunt of the blow.

I was able, with help from several bystanders, to slide the bike to the curb. Of course this was long before the coming of cell phones. Through the police radio system we were able to contact our roommates, who came to pick us up.

Wow, what had been a really pleasant ride and conversation with a good friend, over a cold draught of beer, suddenly became a near tragedy. We both could very realistically have been killed that night. Fortunately, my friend John fully recovered from his injuries.

The man driving the truck was a middle-aged guy who had been arrested for drunk driving a number of times. He had no money and no insurance. I was able to get the bike repaired, and continued riding it for another year prior to selling it. One might reasonably believe that would have been the end of my love affair with motorcycles. That, however would be wrong. In addition to the TR6, I went on to own eleven Montesas and one Maico, all dirt bikes, and one Honda 750 street bike.

Each motorcycle provided me with many experiences, some exhilarating, some not. Suffice it to say I am both happy and lucky to be alive today.

Mostly Montesa

After graduating from the University of Iowa in 1967, I followed Horace Greeley's advice to "Go West Young Man." To be exact, my manifest destiny was Los Angeles, California. There I discovered to my delight the United States importer of Spanish Montesa motorcycles. The store was located on Beverly Boulevard, near where I worked. I admired their trials bikes, Motocross racers, 360cc Monster machines, and King Scorpions. I found myself in Nirvana.

The two brothers that owned and operated the business sponsored some of the best up and coming young TT and Motocross racers in the business, people like John DeSota, known as the "Flying Hawaiian." Wow! TT refers to Tourist Trophy—those motorcycles are street-legal. Motocross refers to off-road motorcycles, those that race on enclosed off-road circuits, on terrain of gravel, dirt, mud, or grass.

Within a few months of daily passing the Montesa importer, I succumbed to temptation, and purchased a new 250cc King Scorpion motorcycle. It was street- legal, with headlight and tail light. This bike afforded me good, and not so good, experiences at Motocross races. I also rode the hill and mountain trails that were found all over Los Angeles, San Fernando Valley, and the high deserts of southern California.

In actuality, my King Scorpion was not an excellent street bike, nor was it a really good off-road bike. It was heavy, weighing three hundred pounds. However, it was pretty much "state of the art" for that point in time. I was able to conquer the fear of riding down steep grades at high rates of speed. Experienced off-roaders said,

"Downhill is just like riding on level grades, except you go faster." Hmmmm.

For me it really was experiential. Once I realized that I could control the bike better by applying more throttle, and less or no brake, I could literally "fly" a good share of the ride. When I began to be comfortable riding very steep and rough terrain, I hungered for a lighter, more powerful machine. Over the years motorcycles did become lighter, and more powerful, with far better suspension.

As it turned out, after a cycle had been raced a season, the distributers would make completely refurbished racing bikes available, at an attractive price, to certain lucky individuals. Remember my childhood Whizzer? Refurbished worked for me. I understood refurbished.

I began Motocross racing at an advanced age—the ripe old age of twenty-eight. I was living in Redondo Beach, California, at the time. I was not a professional factory-supported racer. My racing was strictly a personal passion.

This story takes place at my favorite track—Saddleback, in Orange County, east of Anaheim. Picture this:

Thirty to forty racers mounted on their steeds, lined up side-by-side at an iron pipe starting gate. All bikes fully revving up, waiting for the gate to drop. Then they're off! Racers head for the first turn at full speed. As luck would have it, I get the "hole shot" and lead the entire horde of bikes into the first turn. Then I commit a racer's cardinal sin—I take a brief glance back. That always slows you down. Everyone's bike throttles are wide open. The rider on my left gains...then passes me. As he does, he hits my handle bar. My bike immediately falls. I'm thrown in front of thirty plus motorcycles. They can't stop. They can't veer. Some run over me.

Well, that could have been the end. The ambulance guys are on the track pronto, putting me on the stretcher. The hospital determines I have eight broken bones in my shoulder and left arm. They put me in a cast and discharge me. That night I return to the hospital because my arm is swelling and needs more room in the cast.

I did fully recover from that event. I was up and back to work on Monday. I must be a fast healer, because the cast was off in six weeks, and life was pretty much back to normal.

One would think that anyone who had experienced an event of that nature would say "been there, done that" or "sayonara" to Motocross racing. I didn't!

Most will agree that I have lived through a number of potentially catastrophic experiences. The events my body has survived and recovered fully from are also utterly amazing.

I was a faithful "Viva Montesa" rider and racer. I continued my loyalty to the Montesa importer. Makes me just a bit overwhelmed to reflect upon the amount of time, effort, and treasure that I dedicated to my very strong passion for riding, spectating, and racing motorcycles. From 1964-1985 I owned eleven Motocross motorcycles—mostly Montesa.

Ed Popelka

Mary Henkels Rhiner

Mary is a mother, sister, aunt, reader, writer, traveler, teacher, golfer, gardener, cook, decorator, and outdoor adventurer. Since her retirement as a professor of hospitality from Kirkwood Community College, Mary finds that writing family memoirs has become a passion. As the designated family historian, she enjoys researching ancestry, preserving artifacts and photos, and writing stories that honor past generations.

Mary has hosted over fifteen international students from countries in the middle east, far east, and central America. These cultural experiences have brought additional value and respect for all involved. Mary is pleased to share these memoirs with present and future readers. She hopes that the richness of family life will prevail in your hearts.

The Wild American Women

What a blast! What a gas! What a freakin' screamin' weekend! These were the sentiments of seven courageous women who said, "Yes." Yes, to a zip lining and white-water rafting adventure on the Menomonie and Peshtigo Rivers in northern Wisconsin during July 2017.

Of course, we were guided by several young hunks, any of whom could pass for a son, grandson, or in our dreams—boyfriend. They were good looking, muscular, tanned, friendly, and very patient and encouraging. They were inspired by the outdoors and eager to share their joy and skills with us. Most were college students working a summer job and living in a car, van, or tent. For us, they saved our weekend by turning nervous, apprehensive sixty-year-old women into conquering and wild adventurers.

Upon arrival and check-in, the staff wrongly assumed we were part of a bachelorette party, and they were so excited that we chose Wildman Adventure Resort for our weekend event. Not knowing quite how to respond, and not wanting to lower their expectations, we decided to play along. I never lied or made up so many stories in my life. And, the difficulty in this behavior was trying to remember which story you told to which person. But I will tell you that the story I am writing today is all true.

The seven friends were brought together on Friday evening from North Dakota, Minnesota, and Iowa. We arrived happy, excited, and hungry. So the first order of business was finding a restaurant for dinner. Being in the north woods, dining was limited to a few bars serving mostly locals. Naturally the place with the largest number of cars in the parking lot must be the best. Decision made.

The fresh fish was tasty and came with potatoes and slaw washed down with cold beer. The waitress not only served us, but laughed with us, and interjected her advice, "Don't get married." The interior of the restaurant had a cabin-like atmosphere. It was decorated with deer heads and mounted fish, hinting at large fish tales. We celebrated with a gift of the skimpiest black lingerie for the bachelorette. Now you might wonder how this gift appeared on this scene. Well, it has been the joke of previous adventures of this group, and tends to travel with us, appearing at the most inopportune times. As the designated bride, I accepted it with embarrassment and pleasure.

Our cabin included three bedrooms, five beds, one sofa bed, a blow-up mattress, one bath, and a modest kitchen that served us well. Catered meals were delivered to our doorstep throughout the weekend. These foods were surprisingly tasty, filling, and most welcomed. We had brought our own snacks and adult beverages. We had all the amenities we needed, including plenty of toilet paper.

Zip lining was the first adventure Saturday morning. We rode in a refurbished school bus to our start point. There we were fitted with harnesses—straps and buckles around and over our bodies, and between our legs. We were given a helmet, and gloves with leather palms to slide against the rope to slow us to a stop. All this to assure the safety of our endeavor—and I believed everything they told us.

Our first lesson involved climbing onto a two-foot box and sliding down a twelve-foot rope at a leisurely pace. This was nothing compared to swinging from forty-foot towers at twenty miles an hour with nothing to stop us except the friction created by one leather glove. There was a total of five runs, each one increasing in length and intensity. On the first run I grabbed the rope too hard and came to a sudden stop, and had to pull my body to the tower—a feat requiring considerable arm strength. I never knew I could pull that hard. On the second run, I again grabbed the rope too tight, then let go a little, and crashed into our guide standing on the tower. He took it in stride.

I cannot remember the third run, for by this time I was counting down, "How many are left?" On the fourth run, I grabbed the rope with both hands to stop, and found myself spinning around. Finally, on the fifth run, the guide arranged the ropes to automatically stop me as I got close to the last tower. So I relaxed during this last ride, only to experience a sudden jerk of my body about ten feet from the last tower. Fortunately, the rope gradually brought me in. If I go zip lining again, I will inquire about stopping mechanisms before I sign up. All in all, it was a scary and challenging adventure.

After a tasty lunch, we loaded into another old school bus to take us to the launch site on the Menomonie River for our rafting trip. Gearing up with life jackets, helmets, and paddles, we stepped into our group raft. Now, I had been rafting before, and knew well enough to take a seat in the back for a calmer ride, and was perfectly content to let the newbies in our group take a front seat. There were no hooks for our feet, but we tucked our toes under the seat ahead of us so we would not fall out during turbulent times. Perhaps "tucked" is not the most appropriate word—more like smashed, squeezed, or crushed. Now I understood why they insisted on closed-toe water shoes.

The first part of the river was relatively calm—enough time for our guide to give us instructions as we floated down. There were so many terms for using our paddles—forward, backward, easy, stop, and beast. "Beast" was the term that seemed the least likely that we would use, meaning you paddle as fast and hard as you can. I was worried that I would not be able to remember all these instructions. As it turned out, once we entered the rapids, "beast" was the only command I remember hearing.

As we hit the Class 4 rapid, the highest and fastest on the river, I cringed when I saw the raft ahead of us disappear into the seven-foot drop. This is where the thrill seekers would thrive on an adrenaline rush. For me, it was a controlled panic. I did not want to admit my fears. But it was over so quickly, and I did not have time to catch my breath before we were on the shore—safe and sound.

But that feeling did not last long. We walked back a short half-mile upstream on the Michigan side of the river, only to find another raft to do it all over again. Even though I knew what to expect this second time, the apprehension and nervousness returned in full force. But I do have to admit it was more of a thrill the second time, and I wanted to share in the hoots and hollers by others, but labored breathing to calm myself seemed to take priority.

The next morning, we were preparing for another rafting run on the tamer Class 3 rapids of the Peshtigo River. However, this time we had to run the rapids individually, each in our own inflatable kayak, on our own for paddling and decision-making. The guides would be kayaking near us, helping, or should I say rescuing. Again the river was calm at our launch point—more of a float. The calm turned into easy waves and constant moderate paddling. I was quite content, thinking this would work for me until I learned we were only at Class 1. I had already found my thrill and was perfectly content to stop. But there were six Class 3 rapids to come. After the first one, I began to count down. The guides signaled us to pull our kayaks to the shore after each rapid for instructions on how to get though the next rapid. The main point I remember was keep paddling, because the more you control your kayak, the less likely the river will control you. "Oh, my poor arms," I whispered as I wished I had spent more time in the gym.

I heard screams from several fellow kayakers—some screams were thrilling, but I could tell some were fearful. For me, there were no screams—only prayers. About halfway down the river, I looked ahead only to see an empty floating kayak, and one of our bachelorettes climbing the rocks to get to the shore. Oh my, it was Julie and Sheila from our group. I thought I should go and help, but saw the two guides to the rescue. While they were helping them, I thought to myself, "Who is helping me?" As my kayak started to pick up speed, I quickly remembered my instructions to keep paddling, and realized I was truly on my own. The last rapid was about a four-foot drop and I paddled through with all my might. The shock threw the top half of my body straight back. I popped straight back up in seconds. It was probably the fastest sit-up I ever did in my life.

Again the group was pulled over to the shore for more instructions. As I approached, I wondered why everybody was getting out of the kayaks, and suddenly realized the trip was over. With helping hands I crawled out of the kayak onto the rocks. I had a big smile, but my knees were shaking. I was relieved the designated bride had survived. My knees had not shaken that much since my first wedding.

Summersalt

He was small in stature, barely over five feet tall, and almost just as wide. He was a painter by craft and a cook by hobby. In his later years, after the death of his wife, he moved to Dyersville, Iowa, and lived with his sister, Ida Lippert, who was my grandmother. He had no children. His name was Henry Summer, and he was my great uncle.

Henry had a passion for cooking, and occupied my grandmother's kitchen with his concoctions, trials, and tasty treats. The main tool of his passion was a set of knives that he treated as his children—constant attention, extreme care, protectiveness, and a great sense of pride and accomplishment. His sharpening tools were kept in the basement. You would often find him there caring for his knives. In later years, after he died, you might hear family members saying, "Oh, use Uncle Henry's knife." Everyone knew to exactly which knife you were referring.

He was a bit eccentric in that he insisted that you had to have the "BEST" of everything—a special brand, a unique recipe, and even a special paintbrush. His father owned a carriage business and Uncle Henry painted detailing on the carriages. He used a striper brush that could paint straight lines in record time with great precision. He was one of few people in the area with this skill. He also expanded my grandmother's garden to include chokecherries. These are sometimes called "bitter berries," and their unique flavor made the best quality jam.

He loved limburger cheese, and we often kept our distance from him and the kitchen when he served this cheese—to himself. One December my cousin decided to buy her Christmas presents before the college break, and she purchased limburger cheese for Uncle Henry. This created quite a predicament in her suitcase, affecting her clothes and other presents for the family. Unfortunately, there are some things we have to learn by experience. We laugh about this now, but her mother never laughed.

In Uncle Henry's later years, he created a "secret" seasoning, using a mixture of herbs and spices, which he used religiously on meats, poultry, fish, potatoes, and vegetables. He swore the flavor enhanced all culinary creations, but he refused to share the recipe. When asked about it, he offered no hints and simply said, "Well, it's called Summersalt."

Henry Summer passed away in the spring of 1971 and his namesake Summersalt seasoning recipe died with him. Or did it?

Forty years later, I, Mary Rhiner, his great niece, wanted to create a family recipe book. Searching through my mother's recipes (Grace Henkels) I came across a small paper with a handwritten list of ingredients. It was Uncle Henry's writing. There were no quantities or measurements for each ingredient, but the word Summersalt, in my mother's handwriting, was listed at the bottom of the paper. The secret revealed.

To duplicate the special seasoning presented quite a challenge. There were four herbs and nine spices, including garlic and onion. Where to begin? The assistance of a professional chef with a keen sense of smell and taste buds that could enhance any food with flavor was consulted. Since the recipe was created in the 1950s, the flavor enhancer, monosodium glutamate, was eliminated. Also plain salt was reduced, keeping in mind modern day preferences for reducing sodium in the diet. Several trial runs, practice with actual foods, reviews by friends, and eventually Uncle Henry's secret seasoning was recreated.

The seasoning is now prepared, bottled, and shared with friends of the family. It has become a special gift, not only at holidays, but shared with those who like to cook. Or perhaps it is shared with those who will not take money for a special favor. Or it may accompany a dinner invitation, instead of a bottle of wine for the host. Many who receive Summersalt ask for more. One friend hides it in her cupboard so her sister cannot find it. Another uses it on the rim of a Bloody Mary. Others simply smile when a dinner guest comments on the great taste of the food served. Some say with encouragement and conviction, "You need to label, market, and sell this." But my favorite comment came from a cousin, who grew up in Dyersville and knew my great uncle. She said with a smile while reminiscing,

"Oh, it even smells like Uncle Henry."

Written in honor of my great uncle Henry Summer (1885-1971).

The Last Supper

It had been well over a year since my father's cancer diagnosis. His days were filled with hospital and doctor visits, medical tests, and in-home care nurses. We became familiar with patches and pills for pain, oxygen, high-protein shakes, custards, and oatmeal. There were also many visits from his children, family members, and friends. Wednesdays were spent with Bud, his best friend, and Thursdays with Howard, his neighbor. There was reminiscing about his early childhood, his World War II service, his marriage to my mother, his career, and my mother's death. There were also discussions about books he was currently reading in preparation for his death.

One book, in particular, seemed to capture his attention. *Tuesdays with Morrie* by Mitch Albom became an inspiration for him. There was a recurring thought in the book that became a theme statement for him. He would pretend a small bird was on his shoulder and he would turn his head and say, "Is it today, little bird? Is it today?" Of course, there was never an answer, but he knew the end was near. My father had taught me how to live but in this last year, he taught me how to die with peace and dignity.

There were four at the dinner table that evening: Florence, my stepmother; Jim, my brother; my father; and me. We were eating in the kitchen, a more casual atmosphere, compared to the typical family dinners in the dining room. Lasagna, leafy green salad, and garlic bread were served, a far cry from the typical foods over the past few months. But, no wine. Typically wine was a staple for dinner in the Henkels' home, but with my father's diagnosis and medications, it had not been served for over a year. We sat down, recited grace before the meal, and began to eat slowly without a word.

Suddenly my dad said, "I would like some wine."

The immediate response was, "Oh my God, Bob, you cannot have wine with all those medications."

There was silence as he dropped his chin and lowered his eyes without protest. The silence continued as three of us looked at each other, then turned our eyes to dad.

Jim said, "I'll get the bottle."

At the same moment, Florence said, "I'll get the opener."

So we poured a small glass of wine for each of us. My dad's serving was only a few ounces, still he was grateful. He took one sip, then another; however he did not finish the wine. I am sure it did not taste good to him, but he did not complain.

Within thirty-six hours, he had passed away. It was comforting to know that we honored a simple request from a dying man.

A few days later, right after the funeral, about thirty family and friends gathered at the house. We decided to toast my dad by sharing the wine that was left from the same bottle served at his last supper. We crowded into the kitchen and watched as my brother poured a little bit of wine in everyone's glass while he told the last supper story.

There were skeptical comments from some in the crowd, "There won't be enough."

"You'll never make it."

"I gotta see this for myself."

My brother, sharing his Catholic faith and wisdom simply said, "The Lord did it for the loaves and fishes, and He'll do it for this bottle of wine."

And there was plenty for all. We lifted our glasses in honor, respect, and love for a man who touched many lives. My brother looked around the room to be sure to be inclusive of everyone, and looked at each one of us as he said,

"Here's to you, Dad, a loving father, husband, grandfather, great-grandfather, brother, brother-in-law, godfather, uncle, great-uncle, cousin, neighbor, and friend." And we all smiled and nodded in appreciation of the gift we had received.

The empty wine bottle was repurposed into a lamp, with a plain brown shade and a little bird resting on the top rim. "Yes," said the little bird, "It is today."

Witten in honor of my father, Bob Henkels 1918 - 2000

Breakfast with Father Bill

He was sitting in his wheelchair by the window when I first arrived, unaware of my presence, or even the fact that I was planning to visit. I had called the nurses' station ahead of time. When I called his name, he immediately lifted his head and looked at me.

I said, "It's Mary, your niece, from Iowa."

He smiled and was pleasantly surprised—perhaps shocked—was a better description.

"All the way from Iowa," he said. He couldn't believe it.

You see, he is a Benedictine monk, an ordained priest, who taught for many years at St. Anselm's Abbey, a very exclusive Catholic boys' middle and high school in Washington, DC. He taught math and physics. During his teaching years, our family only saw him for his two-week vacation to Iowa every summer. He was now ninety-one years old and residing at Carroll Manor Nursing and Rehabilitation Center in Washington. He is my dad's brother and one of two living relatives of that generation.

I visited him every morning during our stay. Our conversations were about old times, growing up in Dyersville, Iowa, his current health, the family, and our museum visits. He was not much of a talker—never was—but answered every question I asked. At one point, I asked him how old he was.

He answered quite firmly, "I am forty-five."

I asked him if he remembered Florence, my dad's second wife, and he did. I told him we had recently celebrated her ninety-sixth birthday.

He thought about that for a minute and commented, "Well, she is a *lot* older than me."

Another day, later in the week, I asked him about the year he was born, and he instantly told me, 1924. I told him this was 2016.

Being a math teacher, he paused, looked at me and said, "Well, that math just does not add up."

He did remember that Tim, his sister Louise's son, lived in California, and his brother Paul had a daughter, Sue, who lived in Kansas. He remembered my brother Jim in Iowa, and my sister Annie in Tennessee. But every time I asked him about the next generation of children in the family, he said he remembered but *vaguely*. Vaguely seemed to be a response for many things.

Each morning when I came to visit, he was eating breakfast. I sat with him and assisted as needed, but he managed quite well on his own. A few times I turned the plate to make it easier for him to scoop the food. Each day he wanted to hear all about the museums we had visited the previous day. He seemed to enjoy the conversation and was excited when I told him we saw Julia Child's kitchen, Abraham Lincoln's hat, and Benjamin Franklin's walking stick.

I knew he had vision problems, macular degeneration, but he said he could read. I knew he had hearing issues in the past, but that did not seem to affect our conversation. He was always in his wheelchair, and he said he could walk, but I never saw him walking.

He was always well dressed, clean, and neat. He ate most of his breakfasts, but commented that the sausage did not taste like Iowa sausage. He loved his high protein shakes, toast that he could pick up with his fingers, and the hot cereals that stuck to the spoon, and slid down easily. Eggs and meat took longer to chew. So breakfast often lasted over an hour.

One morning I told him that it was time to catch my bus. He said that he was leaving also.

I said, "Where are you going?"

He said, "Going to Dyersville, where I grew up."

The staff was attentive, pleasant, and truly enjoyed his company. He was always alert and in a pleasant mood. They called him "Father Henkels." Every time he was helped, whether it was taking his pills, eating his food, or taking his blood pressure, he would thank them. He was always so cooperative and appreciative of their help.

During our week-long stay, I visited him every morning, except for one day when we had to meet the boat at eight in the morning for our Potomac river excursion to Mt. Vernon. I told him I would not be visiting on that Tuesday.

When I arrived Wednesday morning, the first thing he said to me was, "You were not here yesterday."

That told me how much he looked forward to my visits. During our time together, I read him stories about the family. We prayed together. I gave him smiles, gentle touches, hugs and kisses. On the last day, tears were held back by both of us. Just before I left, he gave me something very special. *He gave me ... his blessing.*

Father Bill Henkels passed away in January 2017.

Sally Stejskal

Sally was born in Cedar Rapids, Iowa, grew up there and retired there. She spent most of her working years in the business world in Cedar Rapids except for one year living in California with her husband while he was in the Army.

She was born of an alcoholic father who was a blue-collar worker, but thanks to wonderful educators, strong mentors and a supportive mother and other family members, she was determined to succeed and build a better life for herself. That she did--learning new things all along the way. With her love of reading, she developed an interest in writing. It began with short stories primarily for her local grandson and turned into a story of her life dedicated to all her grandchildren. Included here are a few stories on her life experiences and lessons learned the hard way.

Sticky Fingers

In the early years of growing up, my best friends, were from the neighborhood. We all went to the same one-room school and we all lived within walking distance of one another. One friend was a couple of years older than I, and she and her younger sister lived just across the road from us. As we grew a little older, probably nine or ten, our boundaries began to expand beyond the immediate neighborhood. Janet, my older friend, was allowed to go to the movies downtown without parental supervision. One Saturday she invited me to go along. Janet was so much more experienced in the ways of the world. She gave me my first haircut when I was little.

I was so excited to be allowed to go with her, and was given a small allowance to do some shopping at McLellan's dime store, pay for my movie ticket and even get a treat at Woolworth's soda counter, another downtown dime store. Her mother gave us a ride to the theatre, and told us what time and where she would pick us up. Wow, we were on our own—quite an adventure for me. Feeling all grown up, into the movie we went.

After the movie was over, we walked from the Paramount Theatre to McLellan's dime store to shop. Decals were all the rage at that time—you could put them on lots of things and use them for all kinds of decorating. Remember, I had limited funds to spend so Janet explained we could buy one or two decals, which would give us a sack—then when no one was looking, we could slip some more into the sack without paying for them. I didn't think this was a good idea, but she convinced me no one would know, and we would have all the decals we wanted. Okay, I said, and we proceeded with our plan. I thought it was a bit risky, but the plan worked, and we left the store to wait for our ride home.

Upon arriving at home, I proudly showed my mother all the decals I had acquired and explained how I was able to get so many. She was horrified with what I had done and told me I was a thief and could go to jail for stealing. She promptly put me in the car to take me back to the dime store to pay for the decals or return them and fess up to my crime with the store clerks. I was terrified walking into the store but knew I had to clear my name. Shaking in my boots, I walked up to the counter where the decals were being displayed and when no one was looking I sneaked them from my sack back onto the counter. As I completed the task I set out to do, I felt a big sigh of relief at not being caught and sent to jail. I quickly left the store and joined my mother waiting in the car to return home. We didn't talk about it anymore and I didn't have the heart to tell her exactly how I solved the problem, but I certainly learned an unforgettable lesson about honesty.

Sally Stejskal

Overconfidence

I turned eleven years old, and like other students at a certain age, it was time to learn to play a musical instrument. The instrument of choice for Czech families was usually the accordion. I began taking piano accordion lessons at Kinney Studios in downtown Cedar Rapids. The studio specialized in guitar and accordion lessons and was located in a space on second floor of an old building. I can't say I really enjoyed my lessons, but I practiced faithfully and climbed the wooden stairs dragging my accordion in its case up to the second-floor studio each week for my lesson.

I have never been musically inclined. I could not hold a beat, had two left feet, and carrying a tune was way beyond me, but I gave the accordion my best effort until my first recital. I practiced the selected music over and over until I knew it by heart and could play it without mistakes. The recital was held at the Paramount Theatre, so I packed up my accordion, wore my best outfit, and was taken to the theatre by my parents. I did not pack my sheet music in my accordion case since I was confident I knew it from start to finish.

As I waited back stage for my turn to go on, I suddenly realized I could not remember a single note of how to perform the piece I was selected to play. I could not refresh my memory no matter how hard I tried—it was a total blank. I had no sheet music to help me remember. I entered the stage at my turn and tried to force it, pressing the buttons, playing piano keys, and expanding the bellows in and out, but as you can imagine, it was awful, and I was totally humiliated. I don't remember ever having another recital, so I must have given up playing the accordion except for an occasional beer barrel polka for my

parents and their friends. My disastrous stage performance taught me a life lesson about being overconfident.

Sally Stejskal

Getting Fired

I was nine years old and eager to earn some money of my very own. One of my neighborhood friends knew of a truck farmer that hired kids to help harvest their produce. It was strawberry picking season and I quickly signed up, excited to have a real job. We had to walk a little over a mile to the pickup station at the closest high school, where a big truck with high wooden sideboards would come by at 7:00 am to load all the workers and take us to the farm.

Once there, we were given carriers holding six quart boxes to hold the strawberries. We crawled along our assigned rows picking the strawberries. You could eat as many as you wanted, but then your boxes would not fill up as fast. I loved strawberries, so I ate a lot of them. When the carrier was filled, you would take it to the collection station and would be given a ticket for each quart filled, and a new set of empty boxes. At the end of the week, you turned your tickets in for your pay at the rate of five cents per quart.

It was hot crawling on your knees all day in the burning sun, but eating lunch packed in a black metal lunch pail was a pleasant break in the day. A pretty little creek ran through the farm and we would remove our shoes and socks, sit on the bank, and dangle our feet in the water to cool off while eating our lunch. Back to the fields to continue picking until the final call at 5:00 pm to turn in our picks and get our pay tickets. We would then climb back into the truck for the ride back to the school and the long walk home after a full day in the fields.

I remember thinking this was a hard way to make a living—low pay for awfully hard work, and besides, I firmly believed the farm owner didn't like me. I must not have been a fast-enough producer, often sidetracked by baby bunnies in my picking row, or other critters and insects I seemed to find. I even took one of those baby bunnies home in my lunch pail, thinking I could feed it from an eyedropper and raise it to be a pet. My dad warned me it would not work, and he was right. Little did I know that bunny needed his cozy nest and the warmth of his mother to survive.

In any event, why did I think the farmer's wife didn't like me? I was always given the rows previously picked and had the smallest berries, so it took much longer to fill my boxes while the picker "pets" were assigned the newer planted rows with the big plump juicy berries.

As I contemplated this situation over the weekend break and counted my meager pay for the week, I had a great idea on how to increase my production. I could hardly wait to begin my job the following Monday. As usual, I was assigned the oldest and least productive picking row, but I had a plan—fill the bottom of the boxes with straw from between the rows and pick enough strawberries to cover the straw and round off the top of the quart boxes. I quickly filled my boxes and turned my carrier in for my share of pay tickets. I was pleased with myself since I had my most productive day.

At the end of the day before climbing into the truck, the farmer's wife called me over to the collection station, asked for my tickets, paid me and said, "Don't come back." I was fired from my first real job, but I learned a valuable lesson about doing a job properly.

Sally Stejskal

A Bad Habit
Turned Positive

Once I learned how "cool" smoking was back in the college years, I continued off and on until I started my full-time career in the software and data processing industry where I became a chain smoker, burning many cigarettes in the ashtray on my desk. I could even fill up the little ashtrays in the arm of the airplane as I flew back and forth from Los Angeles, Chicago, or Philadelphia. It never occurred to me how badly I smelled and what a horrible habit it was, because so many others smoked as well.

As time passed and smoking became less tolerable to society, I began thinking about quitting. It was one of the biggest and hardest challenges I had faced in my life. My husband's employer began a smoking cessation class and offered it to spouses as well as employees, so I decided to give it a try. By then I had been smoking for almost thirty years and was ready to give it up. The class was conducted by a representative of one of the local hospitals. We met weekly.

As the weeks went by people dropped out, so the final class size was quite small. I entered into a competition with a male smoker as to which one of us could hold out the longest. I was determined it would be me. At the end of class we both had quit, and I have not smoked a cigarette since. I later learned my competitor had gone back to smoking, so I really was a winner.

During the early days being around smokers, and particularly my husband, was difficult, but I was determined to beat this nasty habit. There was a lot of complaining to my husband about his continuing to smoke, but it fell on deaf ears. He did try to smoke away from me, and kept his cigarettes in places out of my sight to help me avoid temptation. My husband continued to smoke until he had a heart attack in 2011 and was forced to quit.

I decided to save the money I would spend on cigarettes until there was enough for me to buy something special. At that time in 1991, the cost of a pack of cigarettes was less than a dollar, compared to current prices of over five dollars. I wanted to purchase a Golden Retriever puppy. We adored the neighbor's Labrador and wanted a bigger dog than our Dachshund. Watching the classifieds, I found an ad for Golden Retriever puppies. I called and negotiated the purchase of a female puppy for one hundred dollars. The owners were teachers from New Hampton, Iowa, and they agreed to deliver her to our flower shop one evening. I met them there, and the little bundle of fur was mine to take home. My husband was not thrilled to have a new puppy, but soon became as attached as I. We named her Nikki after the Nicorette patches I used to help quit smoking.

She loved lying on the upper deck of our acreage house, where she could watch over the countryside. When we moved to town we would get phone calls asking if we knew our dog was on the roof of the garage. She had found a way to climb from a picnic table to a storage shed and onto the garage. We decided to build her a tree house in the yard behind the flower shop, which she enjoyed for many years. My father-in-law would come over every morning to coax her up the ramp with a treat, so she could oversee the comings and goings of the world around her.

We had Nikki for almost ten years when she became ill with cancer. She was the perfect dog, always wanting to please, never soiling in the house, or smearing windows, or jumping on people, or doing other annoying things dogs can have a bad habit of doing. She went everywhere with us, including a trip to Canada. We have had two more Golden Retrievers since then, but there will never be another Nikki. That was the best hundred dollars I could have spent from quitting the terrible habit of smoking.

Federal Grand Jury

What was this envelope addressed to me from the United States District Court? It sent my heart skipping, but upon opening it I learned I was being summoned as a Federal grand juror to the Court of the Northern District of Iowa. There were a number of documents to complete and return, electronically or by mail, prior to reporting in September 2013. I did not have any idea what being a Federal grand juror involved, but I was soon to find out.

Instructions were given as to date and time to report, where to park, and how to pay for parking. Upon entering the impressive new courthouse recently opened overlooking the Cedar River, I was immediately intimidated by the security system in place prior to gaining entrance to the building. The security officers were expecting us, so we were welcomed through the screening process similar to that at airports. Yes, you might have to remove your shoes and some items are confiscated for the day, like cameras and certain electronic equipment. One gal even had her knitting needles taken away.

We were escorted to a large room designed as a welcome center where we were shown a film and given a brief overview of the federal justice system and the duties of a grand juror. We were then escorted to a court room where twenty-three jurors and five alternates were picked. I was not only chosen as one of the twenty-three, but called to the front by the judge along with two others, and asked if I would be willing to act as a foreperson. I thought she said floor person, but quickly figured out the proper terminology. After the main foreperson, I was designated foreperson #1, and the other fellow as foreperson #2, to act in that order if the main foreperson was unable to be present. I only had to act in that capacity once.

The judge read the specific rights and responsibilities of a grand juror, and we were all sworn in. We were introduced to the grand jury room and related facilities, excused for lunch, and told to report back at a time when my life as a federal grand juror for eighteen months would begin.

Tuesday, Wednesday, and sometimes Thursday were set aside each month, generally during the third week. We were given a schedule at least two months in advance. Our days began at 9:00 am and we were usually finished before 5:00 pm. The days would vary depending on the number of cases to be heard and the availability of witnesses for each case being investigated. Cases could involve drugs, firearms, tax evasion, bank fraud, illegal immigration, child pornography, sexual exploitation, murder for hire, bank robbery, and any other crime against the United States government.

The jury room held the full panel of jurors in courtroom style tables and comfortable chairs, since you spent a lot of time sitting. The district attorney sat at the front along with the court reporter. There was a table with a microphone for the witness being questioned. A full set of audio and video equipment completed the mostly soundproof room. Personal electronics, including cell phones, cameras, tablets, were not allowed in the jury room. A set of lockers was provided outside the jury room, along with a kitchenette area with a microwave, a small sink, coffee pot, and refrigerator.

We also had a set of restrooms and a locked filing cabinet to hold our notebooks. The notebooks were used for taking notes on each case, and locked away each night before leaving the area. Paper and dividers were furnished for the notebooks. A box of tissue was usually available on the witness desk, not only for the witnesses, but jurors could help themselves as well.

The courtroom staff and security personnel were all very friendly and did everything they could to make us feel welcome and comfortable in performing our service. There was a break room on the second floor with tables and chairs and a number of vending machines available, but most jurors either ate on premises in the jury room, or went out to eat at local restaurants in the vicinity. We had a minimum of one hour for lunch, and often times more before the next case might be ready for presentation. It would have been desirable if there had been a small table and chairs outside our jury room for those eating in or wishing to read using an electronic device, but the jurors' suggestion never came to pass.

The foreperson was responsible for swearing the witnesses in, and if a case was ready for an indictment, reading the charges, asking for discussion and a vote. During discussion on the indictment, the attorney, court reporter, and any law enforcement personnel left the room. A vote of sixteen jurors was required for probable cause to move forward on a case. Some cases were short with only one or two witnesses and could be concluded immediately. Others could run for several months and required many witnesses before being asked for an indictment. We had a number of cases that did not get presented for indictment at the end of our term of service. Those cases were passed on to the next panel of jurors.

There could be a lot of time between cases or witnesses, so patience was a virtue. We learned not to expect every case to move along smoothly. After all, we were dealing with criminal cases, so we had to expect the unexpected. Even the attorneys would occasionally have to deal with the unexpected.

With the same panel of jurors meeting for eighteen months, a bond of friendship and respect developed. We each had our own personalities, jobs, and activities, whether active in the job market or retired. We looked forward to meeting each month, eager to learn what cases would be on the docket for the day. We became familiar with the attorneys and learned which ones specialized in certain types of cases. We learned the strengths of each attorney presenting his or her case.

I will miss the monthly sessions and the people involved. It was a real learning experience about our judicial system that I tremendously enjoyed. I am happy I had the opportunity to serve in a capacity I never would have dreamt of doing. I hope everyone notified of possible jury selection will look at it as a positive experience.

Patti Thacker

"The girl next door" writes with joy and complete abandon. Growing up in Dubuque, Iowa, she moved to Cedar Rapids in the mid-sixties to "seek her fortune" at the famous Killians department store as a copy writer in the advertising department. A series of promotions resulted in being named "fashion coordinator," the most coveted job of all.

From her first step on the runway at the age of three she knew fashion was her passion. Many trips to New York afforded numerous opportunities to meet world-famous designers and celebrities as well as taking in the glorious sights and sounds of the Big Apple. The following years have brought even more occasions to visit other fashion capitals of the world—mainly London and Paris. What bliss! Who knows what tomorrow will bring!

My Obsession With White

I like to imagine my obsession with white began with an extended stay in the pristine preemie nursery of St. Joseph's Mercy Hospital in Dubuque, Iowa, under the watchful eye of director of the school of nursing, Aunt Catherine Elizabeth Tully.

Upon release, my twin sister and I were immediately escorted to St. Anthony's Catholic Church to receive the holy Sacrament of Baptism. Cradled in the arms of loving aunts and uncles, once again the ubiquitous color white was front and center due to elegant attire accomplished by the collaboration of Aunt Bess' proudly handmade linen dresses and bonnets combined with the exquisite lace embellishments provided by the crochet hook of Aunt Vickie Kelly.

First Holy Communion provided yet another opportunity to add one more white item to my wardrobe. I clearly remember saying to my mother, "Mummy, I am going to wear this beautiful dress and veil when I get married"—begging the question—was I not going to grow any bigger or were they going to grow so that this could possibly happen.

Eighth grade graduation, combined with the crowning of the Mary Queen of May ceremony, dictated white dresses and pale blue satin sashes for all girls involved.

First prom at Immaculate Conception Academy brought forth an entirely new meaning to the words "awesome moments." Three sets of twins in our class created a heart-stopping moment—all had chosen the exact same dress! Could this be possible? YES, YES, and YES. Ours were white—theirs peach and pink! Crises averted!

The best white dress of all was the creamy white slipper satin delight with silk illusion flyaway veil that I wore on a beautiful sunny Saturday morning at Immaculate Conception Church when I married the love of my life—John Luke Thacker.

White still continues to make my heart smile—my fifty shades of white in my home at Blair House, the glow of the first morning star that assures me my beloved is truly in heaven, the shimmering beauty of a pearlescent full moon on a warm summer night, or choosing an elegant white mandevilla for my terrace. Last of all, the much-anticipated excitement of the symphony in white arrival of my adored and adorable ninety-five-year-old mentor, LaBelle Lipsky from her winter home in Sanibel Island, Florida in June melts my heart like a candle!

Patti with LaBelle Lipsky

Hats—Hats—Hats

From the first moment I caught my reflection in the mirror, the "magic" of wearing a hat began. The life-long love affair was in full bloom!

Easter Sunday brought forth a crisp straw bonnet and summer days ahead would provide a parade of colorful gingham sunbonnets that matched the prerequisite sun suits worn on hottest summer days.

One of my favorites in my back to school wardrobe was a bright red felt Dutch girl creation with dainty flowers and white buttonhole stitching all around the edge.

Winter brought on another "new look"—something called a parka hood in luxurious mohair that tied under the chin to insure added warmth. It had an enormous scarlet tassel on top that bobbed and flipped around as I walked or ran about. It was a favorite until my friend Mary Elaine Jungle showed up with her favorite cover-up, sporting a ring of fur around her beautiful face. To this day I am still pea green with envy about that.

My mummy had a milliner, Stella Marr, who had a shop on 11th and Main. She provided our hats all through my high school days until I grew up and came to Cedar Rapids to start my life-long career at Killian's.

The store provided an endless array of millinery delights. There was something for every season and occasion, whether from the hat bar or haute couture collection by Alyn Lethbridge, Adolpho, Halston, Schiaparelli, and many other designers. Cedar Rapids gave us our own "Ethelberta," a lovely, talented, and creative milliner, whose breath-taking beauties made the scene at society weddings, cocktail parties, football games, and business events. I was blessed to be named her model extraordinaire and I loved it.

One particularly favorite hat of mine is a beautiful leopard-print straw hat from the world-famous Selfridges in London. It was worn and loved by Fred Astaire's gorgeous and glorious dancing partner, the beautiful Ginger Rogers. It was purchased and won in a four-way bidding war by a very special friend benefitting the animal shelter in Palm Springs, California.

I have collected and worn mouth-watering chapeaux from New York, London, Paris, Honolulu, and dozens of other cities in between.

The most exciting treasure of all is this yummy hat from Galeries Lafayette in Paris. I absolutely adore this face framing beauty in a luscious strawberry pink accented by an enormous silk peony in the center. It is fun to wear and always brings forth smiles of joy and delight.

One day, if it is in God's plan, "Celestial Hats" will be my store of choice. Will I have the usual basic halo? Absolutely not! I am thinking about something made with gleaming stars, creamy white pearls and brilliant white diamonds. You can be sure it will be heavenly!!!

Classy Bailey Boot Shop

I was a "sixties" career girl on the move. My dream of becoming a member of the advertising team at the famous Killian's Department Store in Cedar Rapids, Iowa had come true. I was the new copywriter extraordinaire of print, radio, and television.

I was immersed in the world of fashion. Shoes, among other desirable "must have" accessories, became my passion. My wandering eyes ever on the search for the ultimate in desire and design led me to the temple of worship and the sinfully delicious coverings for the foot found at the elite Bailey Boot Shop located in the Guaranty Bank Building on Third Street in downtown Cedar Rapids.

After years of pressing my nose against the glass, I was confidently able to step inside and let the journey begin. The atmosphere exuded beauty all around. There was an unmistakable essence of class in concert with elegance that made my heart skip a beat or two. I carefully perused the most breath-taking collection of beautiful footwear I had ever seen.

I picked up one shoe after the other: a barefoot sandal, a sleek slide, a flattering D'Orsay pump! I felt the silky, smooth leather, and the luxurious cashmere-soft suede creations, in colors to please the most vivid imagination. I made my selection of styles to try on and casually handed them to Mary Cashin, a no-nonsense kind of woman of no particular age, who displayed no outstanding fashion sense. She had a Dutch girl haircut, wore little or no make-up, and was a member of the classic cashmere sweater "set," which was the gold standard of the time. Her shoes were sensible. In spite of this, she flawlessly pointed out the most fascinating selling points imaginable found in the pages of the "universities of print," the famous Vogue or Harper's Bazaar magazines.

My favorite shoe was in my hand! Having heard often the phrase, "If you have to ask, you probably cannot afford it," I held my breath and inquired just how much would it take to make my dream come true.

She looked into my anxious eyes—then back to the sticker on the box. My first paycheck of $35.00, a huge windfall at the time, was still tucked into my purse awaiting deposit at the nearby Merchants National Bank. Fortunately my daddy had provided a cushion of $100.00 to see me through any emergency that might arise—so I was covered should my choice exceed my "cash on hand."

I held my breath—$25.00—a fortune to me and many other working girls in that day. Without missing a beat, and breaking into a zillion-dollar smile, I confidently declared that the shoes in fact would be mine, as though I had done it many times before.

The transaction was complete! With a classy Bailey Boot shopping bag in my hand, I left the store in a heightened state of euphoria. I had indeed arrived!!!

Mr. Straw

Mr. Straw is a sterling presence in my life, a bon vivant, a world traveler with a lifetime passport to everywhere.

Mr. Straw entered the world of timeless travel and privileged luxury upon leaving the elegant confines of the world-famous jewelry store, Tiffany and Company on upper 5th Avenue in New York City.

Traditional luggage was traded for a soft and luxurious sleeve, and the ubiquitous teal blue box tied with a shiny white satin ribbon. He was after all a gift from my adoring and adorable husband, John Luke Thacker.

Mr. Straw's first night was spent at the St. Moritz Hotel at 59th and 6th Avenue before enjoying a limousine ride to LaGuardia Airport for the first of many plane rides that would become his favorite mode of travel to Cedar Rapids, Iowa.

For me it was love at first sight, or should I say sip? We have been inseparable ever since, except for one night of terror....

After spending a birthday celebration evening at the Light House Restaurant with friends, I discovered at mass the next morning, while searching for my offering, Mr. Straw was not in my purse. My heart stopped. It was the one-year anniversary of John Luke's arrival in heaven, and my fragile being was shattered. A call to the restaurant proved to be devastating!

As a distraction, my friend Diane K. Spicer and I went shopping at Von Maur. While roaming the shoe department, I heard one of John Luke's and my most favorite songs being played on the piano: Rainbow Connection. Was it? Could it be a sign? My phone rang at the very same time.

My trembling voice answered with apprehension. Mr. Straw had in fact been found. Outside. In a big dark dumpster. A miracle to be sure, and yet another declaration that JLT would never, never, let me be disappointed and heart broken.

Since then Mr. Straw has enjoyed a life of adventure, seeing sights, and enjoying the sounds of London, Paris, Honolulu, Maui, Giverny, Las Vegas, 5th Avenue, Michigan Avenue, Rodeo Drive, and Hollywood Blvd. He has enjoyed the company of presidents, governors, Hollywood elites, and designers of the most well-known fashion world, as well as jockeys, professional athletes, and noteworthy clergy.

Mr. Straw's vintage provenance makes him even more special and precious. He shines in the light of the sun or the soft gleam of a moonlight night. He is my most treasured possession in all the world, and I will love him dearly forever and a day.

The Sidewalks of New York

Autumn in New York. The perfect season for my introduction to the most exciting city in the world.

It is a sunny Sunday afternoon. The sleek United Airlines plane slowly circles the city. It glides ever so smoothly over the East River heading toward the runway of LaGuardia Airport. We prepare for landing. We extinguish our cigarettes. Yes, we can smoke on the plane. Stewardesses retrieve cocktail glasses. Food and beverage carts are stowed safely away. Seats are put in their upright positions. We are minutes away from stepping onto terra firma. It's wheels down onto the runway, and my heart beats a little faster as the propellers reverse with a roar. The terminal complex is in sight. We roll to a stop at the gate. The stewardesses declare seat belts may be released. We retrieve our personal possessions and begin to disembark.

What seems like forever affords us the opportunity to join the throngs of people heading towards the spinning carousels. They are piled high with luggage in an unidentifiable array of shapes and colors. At last our luggage is in sight. A Skycap hurries to help us retrieve it and rushes us into the endless line of ubiquitous yellow taxis for the rank and file, and sleek black limousines for the privileged executives and assorted glitterati.

A cacophony of familiar and unfamiliar sounds fills the air summoning drivers to the next available pick-up area. Skycap tips are distributed, horns blast, whistles blow, engines roar into life. My two co-workers and I are off to the city in a super-long stretch vehicle provided by the largesse of my adorable, loving husband, JLT, in celebration of my first visit to The Big Apple.

My boss, Deane K. Smith, Ann Roland Kohl, and I speed along Riverside Drive, cross the 59th Street bridge, and view the city skyline. We are just minutes from my new home for the next week—the classy and classic St. Moritz Hotel on the corner of 59th and 6th.

Tonight is free of responsibility. Tomorrow the work week begins. I am here as a buyer and fashion coordinator for Killian's, the premier department store in Cedar Rapids, Iowa. Deane has planned an evening of orientation so that I will at least have a nodding acquaintance of my neighborhood and surrounding area. We check in; then the three of us step out into a world of wonder.

Being the horse lover that I am, the line-up of carriages circling Central Park beckons to me with sheer delight. I make a quick review of the situation and a split-second decision. I step into the corner deli for a bag full of shiny apples for my newly-acquired equine friends. They await a pat on the head and a sweet treat to munch on. Considering the apples cost a dollar apiece, and dinner is yet to be factored in, it is obvious that my per diem is not going to last long. JLT will need to become my financier by noon tomorrow.

Time is of the essence. My must-see list is long, and time is short. My first wish to see the horses has been granted. Now it is on to 5:00 o'clock mass at St. Patrick's Cathedral. Our walk down 5th Avenue reveals Bergdorf Goodman, Tiffany's, Cartier, Saks, the St. Regis Hotel, and the renowned Plaza Hotel. Radio City Music Hall, Rockefeller Center, and other famous hotels and shrines of commerce are now in view.

We reach 40th Street and the Theatre District. The white lights of Broadway illuminate the night sky. Restaurants and bars, large and small, line the streets. I choose Sardi's as a must-do. I hope for a glimpse of a famous face.

With an early dinner out of the way, we head south to a world apart—the Empire State Building, Wall Street, Twin Towers with the elegant Windows of the World Restaurant, Trinity Church, Little Italy, Chinatown, and Greenwich Village. Our modes of transportation were many: cab, bus, or walk. As my adorable Aunt Vickie used to say, shank's mare. We cannot stop now.

My head is spinning. My heart is racing. My excitement and curiosity know no bounds. It's back to the amenities of uptown by way of 7th Avenue and Central Park West. After a quick aperitif at the Tavern on the Green, my dearest wish is about to become true. A sight that I had seen so often was in my lens. A gleaming white carriage. A gorgeous horse and a handsome livered driver await our arrival. Once again, JLT has scheduled and provided the fare for this breathtaking event. We wind our way around Central Park, sharing the joy of New Yorkers of all ages reveling in the beauty of this glorious green space. One more wish has come true.

The busy day is about to close with a nightcap at the famous Carnegie Delicatessen, a legendary watering hole of theatre goers and actors alike. I peruse the menu carefully and make my selection, a ham sandwich on white bread with catsup, and some iced tea. If you can believe it! My order prompts the Brooklyn-born server to blurt out in a loud voice, "For Christ's sake lady, you are sitting in the front window of a world-famous Jewish delicatessen, and you order a ham sandwich? How could you possibly do such a thing?"

People are staring at me. I am embarrassed. I blush sheepishly, raise my head and look deep into his eyes, smile sweetly and say, "Yes sir, I did. Now if you will please bring my order, I am sure we'll all be happy." That brought the house down. I thoroughly enjoy every yummy bite of my ham sandwich.

It is getting late. My whirlwind day is drawing to a close. Tomorrow will be here soon. Will I remember the avenues and streets? Will I find my way to the Eastside, Westside, and all around the town? Or will I find myself standing on a corner of "walk and don't walk" thinking like the old baseball great, Yogi Berra, "When you come to a fork in the road, take it." I cannot wait to see what the day will bring.

John Luke Thacker

The Best Birthday Gift Ever

In the traditional scheme of things, my birthday had developed into a three-week event. No "one and done" mentality here. Being born a party animal, hardly a day went by that there wasn't something to celebrate, or at the very least, acknowledged in some celebratory way.

April 1999 proved to be no exception—morning breakfasts, long lunches, afternoon tea dates, and dinner parties with friends and my beloved John Luke, filled my ever present "dance card."

I was totally delighted to count down the days until the seventeenth—"B"day! Tuesday, the fourteenth, dawned sunny, bright, and beautiful. I "broke bread" with a treasured pal, Margaret Crane Smith, at the Cedar Rapids Country Club.

After a late afternoon check in, John Luke requested a postponement of dinner until tomorrow evening. Request granted! No problem here!

Our early evening share-our-day time came to a complete stop when John Luke went to the kitchen for a glass of water. He asked me to come and rub his back, murmured an, "Oh, baby that hurts," followed by a heart-stopping request to call 911.

Panic overtook my entire being as I took unsteady steps to the nearest telephone. I held him tight as I waited with bated breath for the shrill sound of the ambulance racing up our driveway.

I assured him as best I could that all would be well and that we would be at Mercy Hospital very soon. Blessedly-treasured tender words were exchanged as they proceeded with life-saving measures.

With my devoted friend, Peggy Whitworth, at my side, and dear friend, male-nurse Mickey Siegler in the

ICU, we observed as the clock of life began the countdown to the final minutes, hours, and days of this never-before-witnessed odyssey.

Closest friends, Matt Paul, Peggy Whitworth, Drew McDonald, Megan and Steve Ginsberg, David Bolt, John Stepanek, Jeff Smith, and Larry and Mary Turner, surrounded me with love, care, and concern like no one could ever imagine.

For three days, John Luke's life hung in the balance. My birthday was fast approaching, and my husband's flame of life was dimming more and more each day. The waning hours were a kaleidoscope of emotions. Birthday presents and flowers were piling up at my door, as were telephone calls and written messages from those who had not yet heard the news.

Things were not looking good. The hospital had become my temporary home. Sister Mary Lawrence and Sister Mary Augustine were protective guardian angels that never left my side. Father Gallagher read the prayers of the last rites. I took all of this wonder with a strong and brave heart, and faith that John Luke and God would always, always, take care of me. And, they still do.

A few hours later, the end had come. I walked out of the hospital at dawn's early light and saw in the morning sky the biggest, brightest, and most beautiful star I had ever seen, assuring me that my darling had truly arrived safely in heaven.

It was April 17th, my birthday, and the quintessential April present from John Luke—a diamond bracelet—was on my arm. But the most treasured gift of all did not come in a beribboned blue Tiffany box. It was those three whispered words to me, and me to him, in that fleeting moment before he left me, "Love you, baby." To this day those words send my heart soaring!!!

Anneliese Heider Tisdale

Anneliese Tisdale is the author of two poignant memoirs. In *Christmas Trees Lit the Sky,* she vividly describes coming of age in Nazi Germany. She tells of her family's struggle to survive the war, the fears in everyday life, and the anxiety of having loved ones serving in both the German and the American armed services.

In her forthcoming memoir, *Coming to America*, Anneliese shares her challenges as a German war bride, and of adapting to farm life in southwest Iowa. She reflects upon her journey of becoming a U.S. citizen, her humorous and inspirational path in attaining her BA and MA degrees from the University of Iowa, and the decades she spent as a teacher of Iowa's youth.

Anneliese has been invited to tell her story again and again, at book signings, panel discussions, and within academic settings across the Midwest. Enjoy these excerpts!

Washday

Not long after I, a city girl from Munich, Germany, had arrived on my in-laws' farm near Jefferson, Iowa, I was told it was washday. There was an unwritten law that Monday was washday on the farm, on all farms. Driving down a country road, one could see laundry fluttering in the breeze on farm after farm. This seemed strange to me, kind of regimented. In wartime Germany, due to the scarcity of laundry detergent and the rationing of wood to heat the water, laundry day was limited to once a month. Some hand-washing was done as needed. Not everyone had laundry hanging out on the same day, and it definitely was not always on a Monday.

On my first Monday washday, I did not know what to expect, but I knew I had to carefully observe how things were done in my new country. My mother-in-law, Pearle, had not soaked the dirty laundry in a Persil solution the night before, as was the custom in Germany. A definite plus in my opinion. Nor did we have to make a wood fire under the big cauldron in the basement and then keep it going by replacing more logs, something I had failed to do in Germany on the rare occasions that a fire was entrusted to my care. Instead, pails of soft water from the kitchen pump were heating on the bottled-gas kitchen stove. Another plus.

Soft water was also a new concept for me. I found out this was rainwater that had been collected in a cistern underground to be used for laundry and cleaning. Once the water was hot, it was poured into the Maytag washing machine. Pearle cut a bar of Fels-Naptha soap into the hot water. Next, she pulled the rope on the engine of the gas-powered washing machine several times till it started with a sputter. Soon the pungent smell of the engine mixed with Fels-Naptha permeated the house. The white clothes went into the machine; Pearle moved the lever and the agitator swished the clothes back and forth. After a while, when she deemed the whites to be clean, Pearle used a wooden paddle to get the clothes out of the tub and through the wringer, which was attached with a swivel to the machine. In Germany, Mama had to wring the clothes out by hand, completely exhausting her wrists.

On the other side of the wringer stood a square tub on legs which was filled with cold water for rinsing the soap out of the clothes. After that, they were put through the wringer a second time and placed into the laundry basket.

This was a laundry basket unlike any I had ever seen. Originally it came from the store filled with a bushel of peaches, apples, or pears for canning. By outfitting it with an oilcloth liner with two slits for the metal handles and a wide band that wrapped around the outside top edge of the basket, it now served its new purpose as a laundry basket. A few months later I was to experience another benefit this basket provided. If the basket contained peaches, they were wrapped in squares of tissue paper to avoid bruising them during the transport to Iowa. These tissues were most welcome in the outhouse because they were so much softer than the hard pages of the Sears catalogue or cut up newspapers.

Armed with a large apron-style pouch full of clothes pins, I proceeded outdoors with this versatile basket to hang up the clothes. I admit, I had not done this in Germany, but then how difficult could that be? To my chagrin, my mother-in-law later rehung most of the clothes I had hung out. There seemed to be a definite order.

The sheets, pillow cases, and flat pieces were hung on the clothesline facing the road, while the undergarments and intimate wear were hung on the line behind them, visible from the house but not from the road. While I thought this to be a little odd, the clothesline did appear a lot neater. I watched Pearle carefully so I would do better on future Mondays.

With the white clothes fluttering in the breeze, we started to wash additional loads. The colored clothes followed the whites, then heavy work overalls and jeans, and last of all some throw rugs. I tried to make myself useful, but the first time I ran one of my husband's shirts through the wringer, *ping, ping, ping*, all of the buttons popped off, one by one, before I was able to intervene. I couldn't help but laugh, but this brought a stern look from my mother-in-law. She did not tell me I was stupid—she was not a woman of many words—but I am sure she thought it. I chucked it up to my lack of experience with this new machine and dutifully folded the buttons to the inside on the next batch of shirts, so they could not pop off. Later, I fished the buttons out of the water to be sewn back on my husband's shirt. I was good at sewing and mending. The war and school had taught me that.

The wringer had a bar on top to release it. I did not know this and when I ran my hand through the wringer, not knowing about the release function, I reversed the wringer and ran my hand back through the wringer instead of hitting the release. I counted this as a painful learning experience, not as a negative.

Even though the gas engine smelled, I viewed the washing machine as a great invention. Washday was not an all-day consuming job. In fact, we were done by noon. I considered the gas-sputtering Maytag as a major blessing. I was looking to find all the positives in my new life.

After lunch there was another surprise. I expected that now we would empty the wash water, clean up, and be done. No! The Fels-Naptha wash water now was utilized to scrub the outhouse, a rather disgusting and smelly chore. Definitely not a positive.

The clothes dried quickly in the breezy Iowa June day smelling outdoor fresh and clean. We folded them on the big kitchen table. Those to be ironed were sprinkled with water from a pop bottle with a sprinkler top, then rolled up to be ironed, because tomorrow was Tuesday, and Tuesday was ironing day.

At a Crossroad

In November 1957, my divorce from Bill had become final. Rather than writing to my parents of this distressing news, I wrote to my brother Ludwig and asked him to tell my parents in person. A year later Ludwig came to Jefferson, Iowa, where he spent two months with the children and me. Because my house was very small, my lawyer and friend David, and his wife Madonna had invited Ludwig to stay with them.

It was a busy and exciting summer as we introduced Ludwig to some of Iowa's beautiful scenery, took him to the Iowa State Fair, the Grotto in West Bend, and other attractions. My cousins by marriage, Merle and his wife Signe, enjoyed meeting Ludwig very much, and we were frequent guests at cookouts and tasty Sunday dinners at their farm. As much as I enjoyed all of these activities with my brother, for me, it was most comforting to be able to talk with him about my present unsettling situation and how to go on from here.

Ludwig had relayed my parents' loving and most generous proposal: they had put their house and beautiful large yard in Germany at my disposal. My father inquired and was assured that I would be able to work for the Railroad Administration in Munich again with credit given for the time I had worked there during the war. My parents also offered to take care of my children while I was at work. All I had to do was to say yes, and they were ready to send us tickets for the ship's voyage. They reassured me that no matter what I decided they would be there for me.

After Ludwig returned to Germany, I was left to make what seemed to me an insurmountable decision. I had come to a crossroad—should my children and I stay in the United States or return to Germany?

My thoughts were a pandemonium of pros and cons. While I would be going back to my native country, for my children it would be an all-encompassing adjustment involving a largely different lifestyle, a foreign language, a new school. They were born in the United States. This is their native country. I had been a United States citizen for seven years, and I could not imagine leaving my new country to start up life again in Germany. But how could I stay here and provide a decent life for my children solely on a medical secretary's pay? So far Bill had not paid a penny of the child support payments the court had ordered him to pay.

However supportive my parent's offer was, I felt that I would be going back a failure. My marriage had failed; therefore I had failed. No matter how much I stewed and stressed, I could not come to a decision.

The winter passed, and in the spring of 1959 my parents invited us to come and spend the summer with them in Germany. I gratefully accepted, hoping that this would bring me closer to a decision. On May 28th, the children and I sailed on the MS Berlin from New York.

The ocean voyage was a vacation in itself, and I felt totally pampered. No beds to make, no meals to cook, no dishes to wash, and no worry about keeping within my extremely tight budget. A variety of activities for adults as well as children were planned to keep away any possible boredom. After almost a week of luxury we docked in Southampton, England, for some passengers to disembark and ocean freight to be unloaded. Our next port was across the British Channel, Le Havre, France. From there we sailed on to our final destination, Bremerhaven, Germany, where Papa met us on the dock.

Back row: Anneliese, her parents Elisabeth & Matthias Heider, her brother
Ludwig Heider. Front row: her children, Lorena, Linda, and Larry.

It was a relaxing, incredible summer with my extended family. On long weekends, my brother Ludwig
showed us around Bavaria in his Volkswagen bug, which
the children immediately labeled the "Baby Car" because
of its size. Relatives on both my mother's and my father's
side welcomed and hosted us, and we basked in their attention and love. Neither of my parents spoke English
and the children only knew a little German, but by pointing and motioning they seemed to manage. When all else
failed they came looking for me to translate.

The children were always eager to play with the kids
in the neighborhood, and soon picked up German phrases
while teaching their new German friends the English
equivalent. They loved my mother's German cooking and
some of the new foods to which they were exposed. However, they balked when it came to drinking the lukewarm
milk served in restaurants. They also missed the American hamburgers.

All too soon, it was time to leave for Bremerhaven and the United States. Saying good-bye was heart-wrenching for everyone. Papa accompanied us to the ship, and when the long blasts of the ship's foghorn signaled that it was time for the visitors to leave, the children didn't want to let him go. After a final good-bye, the ship sailed. In less than a week we docked in New York and arrived home in late August.

The children and I were at David and Madonna's for a cookout in the spring of 1960. After dinner we were having coffee while the children played in the yard.

"Anneliese, I know you are still thinking about your parents' offer," David declared. "It is very generous, and a definite possibility should you want to go back to Germany. But you are still agonizing about what to do. Let me give you a plan that will allow you to stay in the United States and give you a future here with an adequate income from a job I think you would be well suited for."

I was stunned as David laid out his well-devised plan: I was to go to college, get a degree and a teaching certificate for German and French. "Foreign language teachers are in great demand," he noted.

"But college is for students fresh out of high school, I have never heard of a divorced woman with three children going to college," I objected. "I'd have to give up my job—what would we live on?"

"I've thought about that," countered David. "Here in the United States, we have a government program called Aid to Dependent Children, ADC for short. You would receive a government check every month to cover your and the children's living expenses. I'm afraid it won't be much, but you could get by on it for four years."

Whenever David started with, "Here in the United States," the unstated message to me was: "You are in the

US now and this is the way it is done here, so for God's sakes, line up."

"But, that is charity," I countered, "I cannot take charity. How could I ever explain that to my parents? No, I would be too ashamed to accept charity."

"Look at it this way, Anneliese. It is a program to help you for a short time. After four years, when you are a teacher, you will pay taxes for the rest of your life. Consider it a loan, because eventually, you will pay it all back to Uncle Sam, every penny of it. So, unless there is another problem, this plan will give you a chance to stay here, if that is what you want."

Perhaps this was the path I needed to take. Trying to make a decision consumed my days and robbed me of sleep at night. I wavered back and forth. By college, I knew David meant the University of Iowa, his Alma Mater. But, the fact was that every time I opened my mouth, people asked me where I came from. Who would hire a teacher with such an accent? No, study at the University seemed out of reach for me. Deep inside, however, I knew I needed to take a chance even if it did sound too good to be true.

A few weeks later, the phone rang and David informed me, "I have the forms for taking the college entrance tests. Come over this evening and we'll fill them out and send them in. Just because you take the tests does not mean you have to go to college."

The day of the tests arrived. A barrage of contradictory feelings accosted me—nervous, excited, hopeful, discouraged. Walking into the room where the tests were to be given, I felt like an oddity amidst this sea of young, bright, and shining faces. At thirty-two, divorced, and with three children, I felt old and out of place.

An efficient-looking woman came into the classroom and read instructions at a rate much faster than I could comprehend: "Your time starts now, open your booklet to page...." Opening the booklet, I saw the questions and beneath each question there were the letters a, b, c, and d. Question after question in the same way, but no place to write an answer. Stuck in the booklet I found a sheet with numbers and rows of circles. I wanted to look around to see what the other applicants were doing, but was afraid it would seem like cheating. Having never taken or even heard of a multiple-choice test, it took me a while to figure out what I was to do.

I had barely started when the monitor announced, "Your time is up, please close your booklet and proceed to the hallway. You have a short break before your next test." To me the break seemed like an eternity. The young people stood around in groups having animated conversations. I stood by myself wanting to run out of the building, but I forced myself to stay. The next set of tests was equally intimidating. It was a feeling of total relief when the last test was finally over, even though I knew that I had failed the tests—all of them.

For some time I stayed away from David and Madonna, making up excuses why I could not visit with them. I did not want to discuss my failed tests, or college, or my future. Summer turned into fall. It was the first week of school when Madonna called.

"Anneliese, you've been avoiding us. Can you and the children come over tomorrow night? David is going to grill something. We really need to take advantage of this nice fall weather. It's not going to last forever." I hesitated, but accepted.

David did not waste any time to inform me: "I called the university about your ACT tests, and it seems you have the distinction of having one of the lowest ACT scores ever." He did not seem in the least disturbed by that fact, nor by having to tell me about it.

"So that's settled. I knew that I couldn't go to the University," I cried out, almost relieved.

Undeterred, David continued: "Those low test scores are the result of a culture gap; you definitely are college material. Here is the good part; once you successfully complete a two-year college, the University of Iowa will admit you as a student." Before I could utter any objections David persisted, "I have called the dean of Boone Junior College, and he is aware of your situation. You can start classes on Monday. The Boone Lion's Club has offered to pay your tuition."

My head was spinning with feelings, running the gamut of being encouraged, confident and hopeful, to reluctant and full of self-doubt. Actually, I was scared to the bone. I realized this might be my opportunity to make it in this country. It almost seemed that the decision had been made for me. If I failed, my parents' offer would still be my safety net.

Three days later, on Monday, I started Boone Junior College, a week late. My first class was Social Science. The teacher started talking about the black belt around Chicago. What was he talking about? I knew it was not a belt one wears around the waist. I did not want to ask; rather I hoped that by reading the assigned chapter in the book, I would be enlightened. The next class was Math. I silently pleaded: *Please, please talk a little more slowly, your words run by me so fast that I don't understand a thing you're saying.* My notes were a rambling of unconnected and unfinished words and sentences. Two more classes to go.

Every morning on the drive to Boone, to give myself courage, I belted out the fight song from Bizet's opera "Carmen." Auf in den Kampf, Toreador, siegesbewußt.... (On into the fight toreador, certain of victory.) Why this song? I don't know. I intensely dislike

189

bullfights. Perhaps it was because my brother used to play it on the piano, and I had always been impressed by its bravado. The drive home was the total opposite, lacking song and bravado. It had been another day of frustrating classes, concepts I did not understand, did not know how to spell correctly in my note-taking, and therefore was not able to find in the dictionary.

One night, when my studying was not going well at all, I threw the book down on the desk and started crying in frustration. "Why are you crying, mommy?" my ten-year-old daughter Linda asked. I had not heard her come into the room. "Oh, honey, I guess I am just tired. I am having trouble with my reading ..."

"But you can't give up, Mommy, you always tell us the worst thing we can do is to give up."

Amen. My daughter had just given me some of my own advice. I tucked Linda back into bed and told myself, "Tomorrow will be another day."

Midterms came, and my midterm report showed a D in each of my four classes.

"Well, at least you are consistent," Madonna said when I told her and David about my midterm grades. I told them about the problems I had with my notes and not being able to find the terms in my dictionary.

The next Monday I was summoned to the dean's office. I assumed I would be asked to leave because of my bad grades.

"I have assigned Marilyn S. to be your 'older sister.' She has the same class schedule as you. Marilyn is very bright and most willing to help you," the dean informed me.

It turned out my "older sister" was about thirteen years younger than I, blond, very pretty, outgoing, and, as I soon found out, very popular with the rest of the students. Most important for me, she took excellent notes.

We went to classes together, and between classes compared our notes and corrected the terms that I had mis-
spelled. Now I was able to find those elusive terms in the
dictionary.

"Look, Anneliese, I brought you some blank cue
cards," was Marilyn's greeting the next morning, as she
proceeded to introduce me to the use of cue cards. At
home I wrote out the terms from the day's lectures on one
side and the definitions on the other. Every day I read
some of them until I understood them. Studying was still
formidable, but no longer unsuccessful. I felt I was beginning to learn and understand.

At the end of that first semester, my grade report
again showed consistency. I had worked myself up to a B
in each of my four subjects and no longer felt the need to
sing the fight song from Carmen to gain confidence.

Marilyn also introduced me to her circle of friends.
Those young people accepted me and didn't mind me tag-
ging along with Marilyn at lunchtime and during breaks.
When my children had no school because of teacher-in-
service, this group of students offered to take care of my
children, so that I would not have to miss classes. They
played "Old Maid" with them in the small school cafeteria, taught them games like blackjack, and helped with
their homework. When the parents of one of the students
invited the group out to their farm for a cookout, the children and I were also invited. They even saddled up two
horses for the children to ride. Marilyn not only helped
me become successful with my studies, she also shared
her friends with me.

"Anneliese, you are one of the five candidates for
homecoming queen," Marilyn excitedly informed me as I
arrived one morning for classes.

"Oh, yes, and a prince is coming on a white horse to
take me away," I laughed, thinking she was kidding. I did

not know much about the ritual involved with homecoming. Two days later, when she showed me the article in the local newspaper, I was stunned.

"Well, you certainly don't need to worry about not being accepted anymore. I think maybe the students are trying to totally 'Americanize' you," David chortled when I told him and Madonna about it.

"The queen will be chosen at the Blue and White Alumni Ball. I'm expected to be there, but I don't know what I am supposed to do. I think it might be embarrassing," I ventured.

"As I've told you before, your middle name should be 'worrier.' You just go, dance and have a good time. Soak it all up. Someday you can tell your grandchildren about this."

At the college, it seems there was just one conversation in the hall, and it all revolved around the Blue and White Ball. The topics concerned the gowns everyone was looking at buying, or had already bought, and what beauty parlor was going to do their hair and nails. While I listened, I could not contribute to these conversations. I was a complete novice. This ball obviously was serious business and I needed to get busy; however, buying a new gown was not an option.

My mother's sister, Aunt Katherine, lived in New York. She knew I could not afford long distance telephone bills, so she usually called me. Sometimes, she sent the children and me clothes from some of her friend's children and grandchildren. Now, I needed her help if I was to go to the dance. So this time, I called Aunt Katherine. After I assured her that the children and I were alright, I told her about the Blue and White Ball and my need for the correct attire. Aunt Katherine was sure that her friend's daughter probably had several gowns hanging in her closet that she would not wear again. While I was pleased to hear that, I could not understand why one

would wear a beautiful dress only once. Aunt Katherine seemed excited and all bubbly about her new mission.

Soon a package arrived and, along with some small presents for the children, there were two gowns, one a beautiful royal blue I loved the minute I saw it. There also were long white gloves and a small satin purse that matched the dress. I could not believe my good fortune. I knew that I could borrow a pair of shoes from my cousin Signe. The only thing I needed to buy was a pair of nylons.

The Saturday of the big event arrived. The night before I had polished my fingernails, and now I showered, shampooed my hair, put it up in curlers, and sat under the plastic dryer cap. Today, it seemed to take forever to get the hair dry. Finally, I was dressed and my hair was done. The children were fascinated with the way I looked. They were especially intrigued by the long white gloves with all the buttons on them. Merle and Signe arrived to take the children home with them. I was to come out in the morning and we all would spend Sunday at the farm.

Driving to the Blue and White Ball I was excited but also anxious. Thoughts raced through my head. *Most of the students attending will have a date, I am going alone. Will I be asked to dance, or will I sit with my feet keeping time to the music?*

My heart was beating faster as I walked toward the ball room and heard the music of the live band. The votes had been counted and I truly felt a great sense of relief when Bonnie, one of the other candidates, was crowned Homecoming Queen. Now, I did not have to wonder about what was expected of me; I was able to relax and actually enjoy the dance. The refreshments were nice, but I was always ready to put down my glass in favor of dancing. Many of my friends' dates did ask me to dance. The teacher I had for Public Speaking also came to our table to ask me to dance several times. I especially enjoyed dancing with him because he was my age, an excellent dancer, quite handsome, and he made me laugh.

When the dance was over, I felt a let-down, and like Liza Doolittle in My Fair Lady, I could have danced all night.

On the drive home, I smiled as I thought back to how much I had dreaded to go to college with those bright, shining faces, as I had called them then. I was so wrong. They had accepted me, accent and all, and helped me acquire the tools to be successful in my studies. They had answered questions that must have seemed ridiculous to them. And then, they even elected me as one of their Homecoming Queen candidates. It was like a mirage in the desert that was not real, and would evaporate into nothing upon closer examination. But it was no mirage. It had really happened.

My life had become extremely busy, and at times hectic and frustrating, but most rewarding. I now had a goal, which, more and more, I perceived to be within my reach. The children pitched in, sometimes willingly, sometimes under duress, by helping with the dishes and doing other chores around the house. Often, I felt guilty when I had to tell them that I had to study, and we could not have a picnic or spend an afternoon at the park. The days, weeks, and months seemed to speed by at an accelerated rate and the school year came to a close. I received my second semester's grades, this time A's and B's. I was no longer a freshman but a sophomore.

It had been a totally different life for me, as well as for the children. With college life and learning, my life and my outlook were gradually changing. It was so gradual that I didn't even realize it at the time. I started feeling better about myself, and gained confidence as far as my studies were concerned. I was so busy that even the stigma of the divorce receded into the background of my thinking.

The children and I were ready for summer vacation and some much-needed unhurried time together. Merle and Signe and their sons Gary and Gail came to pick us up on hot summer evenings or on weekends to go swimming at Spring Lake. Sometimes the children and I drove out to the farm to spend the weekend with them. I also had time to do some of the reading my English professor had recommended to the class. My son Larry almost lived at the municipal swimming pool which was located just a block from where we lived, while Linda spent much time at the library and my youngest, Lorena played with her kitten and her friend Sarah. Vacation time went by fast and soon it was time to go back to school.

During the first week of my sophomore year at Boone Junior College, I was again called into the dean's office. Classes had barely started, so I reasoned that this time it could not be about my grades. I had received another tuition scholarship from the Boone Lions Club, and with it the request that I be on their club's program in April. Maybe it was about that. I entered the dean's office and was offered a seat.

Dean Heyen explained, "Boone Jr. College is again offering community programs this fall. Several of the staff will be teaching classes. You are acquainted with some of them from your studies. Mrs. Hartley will teach American Government, Mr. Porter The Twentieth Century Novel, and your French teacher, Mrs. Turner, is going to teach Beginning Conversational French. We have never offered a class in German. Would you teach Beginning Conversational German?"

I was momentarily overwhelmed but quickly agreed. The thought that the dean had enough faith in me gave me courage and confidence to accept this challenge. My first teaching job. Aside from the experience, I would actually earn some money. I couldn't wait to get home to tell my children, and David and Madonna, the wonderful news.

On October 9th, 1961, I started my teaching career with the first session of Beginning Conversational German. My students seemed very interested in learning German and often stayed after class to talk with me about Germany, the culture, and the German language. As much as I needed the money that I earned, the boost this gave to my self-esteem was invaluable. Next to getting my Associate of Arts Degree, this was definitely the high point of my sophomore year at Boone Junior College.

On Thursday, May 31, 1962, I graduated from Boone Junior College. I think that I must have floated across the stage in euphoria, clutching my diploma, while my children, as well as Merle and Signe, were out among the guests.

My next challenge would be the University of Iowa.

My First Book Club Signing

My book, Christmas Trees Lit the Sky – Growing Up in World War II Germany, was released in November 2012. About three months later, sometime in February, I received a phone call from a woman named Leslie who identified herself as a member of a local book club. She told me that the club had selected my book for their next reading and asked where the book could be purchased locally. Leslie also explained that they were hoping I could come for a discussion and book signing. I gave her the requested information and told her that I would be delighted to come.

I did not know what to expect on that sunny day in April 2013 as I drove to the Cedar Rapids address I had been given. This was my first invitation to a book club. Leslie had told me that the members took turns hosting their gatherings. She had also e-mailed me: "Please come hungry, there will be plenty of food." Another plus, I thought, one night I won't have to cook.

Leslie welcomed me when I arrived at the well-kept home in Cedar Rapids. The members arrived, introductions were made, and appetizers were served. Leslie offered St. Anneliese wine, a lovely Liebfraumilch, and beer from Aldi's, a local German grocer. What a nice touch. As we progressed to the meal, I saw there was more to come. The ham was accompanied by a Bavarian potato salad Leslie had made from the recipe in my book. German mustard and other condiments were available. I was delighted and impressed by the thoughtfulness and work this young woman had put into this gathering. Leslie seemed pleased when I told her what a wonderful surprise this was and that she had done an excellent job making the potato salad. If that were not enough, the dessert consisted of Gesundheitskuchen, a type of bundt cake, again from a recipe in my book. Alongside the cake, there were sliced, fresh strawberries topped with dollops of real whipped cream – just like I remembered my mother serving it in Germany before the war. WOW how neat was that!

After dinner, we proceeded to the living room for the discussion and to my delight a variety of German chocolates were passed around. I am a chocoholic and don't keep chocolate around the house except for special occasions. I considered this a very special occasion, so I indulged.

A lively discussion followed, with many questions being raised. From these questions I could tell they not only had read my book but also had informed themselves about the historical and socio-economic background of the time leading up to World War II.

As the discussion was coming to an end, I was curious and asked if their club had a name. The hostess looked at the other members as if to question, "What shall I tell her?" She finally said, "Well, I'll have to explain. When the club was newly organized and we were looking for a name, we were reading Angela's Ashes."

I quickly interjected, "Oh, yes, by Frank McCourt. I also read that, several years ago." Leslie continued, "Oh, great! Then maybe you remember, in the book the author embellishes his sentences with 'feckin' quite a lot. Well, we wanted a different name for our club. So... we're the 'Feckin Book Club'!"

I laughed, as they gave a sigh of relief that this old lady did have a sense of humor. Leslie also was quick to add that 'feck' does not have the same bad sexual connotation as the 'f' word in English.

The evening had passed too quickly, and when I said my good-byes the hostess presented me with a bottle of

St. Anneliese wine and a lovely bouquet of flowers. They also invited me to come back anytime and join them for one of their discussions. Elated and in high spirits I walked to my car in the still, moonlit night with a bottle of St. Anneliese wine and the bouquet of flowers in my arms.

I thought, *it would be a pleasure and so inspiring to belong to a club like this. Even though these women are decades younger than I am, I feel that I have made some new friends.*

A smile comes to my face and I feel warm inside when I think of this, my first so very special book club signing.

The Long Goodbye

Today the mailman delivered the author copy of my book. I had been eagerly awaiting this moment since sending the manuscript to my publisher. The front cover aptly illustrates the book's title *Christmas Trees Lit the Sky*, depicting the red and green flares used by the Allied forces before bombings. The photos are great—even though many originals were over a hundred years old. The typesetting makes the book "easy on the eye." I am elated and so excited. I can't wait to show my book to my husband, Jim. What will his reaction be?

After what seems to be an eternity, it is time to pick up Jim at Milestones, his daycare place. As soon as we get home I show him my book.

"Look, Jim, my book arrived." Jim just nods. I point to my name on the cover, hoping he will recognize "Tisdale," his name I took when I married him.

"Jim, this is the first copy."

He looks at me with uncomprehending eyes. Jim, the man who normally would have been my staunchest supporter, who would have been so proud of me, has nothing to say.

That night, I cry myself to sleep, releasing the hurt, anger, and frustration I feel as this dreadful disease slowly robs us of our life together. I miss my Jim, the fun-loving man who shared my joys and sorrows, who was always understanding and encouraging. That man no longer exists. Jim no longer understands what is going on around him, no matter how much anyone tries to connect with him. He has dementia, the long, heart-wrenching goodbye.

Jeanne Krsek Vogt

Jeanne hails from the rural heartland of America, Atkins, Iowa. Many of her friendships began in kindergar-
ten, carried forth through high school, and are still cherished today. Jeanne is a small-town girl, with a big city
outlook, a broad sense of humor, ready smile, and hearty
laugh.

Jeanne enjoys spinning a yarn from life's everyday
experiences. She was married for over forty years to Dale
before becoming a widow. Together they raised five sons
and a daughter, and built a family business that has several hundred employees.

Today, Jeanne is an adamant volunteer; she serves
as an officer or board member for fifteen nonprofit and
social organizations in Eastern Iowa. She is always on
the ready to experience life's adventures

202

My Box

Reflecting back on the years I've been alive, I believe my experiences originated from a box. It's only been in the last ten to fifteen years that I recall learning the term, "thinking outside of the box."

As a young child I was definitely in the box—
sheltered from the outside world in a rural area with adult neighbors a half-mile at the closest. I dutifully learned and obeyed all the rules.

Starting school I began peeking out of the box.
But the school years ended with me safely in the box.
The box lid raised a little more at college.

In the work world the lid was open most of the time.

Married and raising a family, plus starting a business, found me outside of the box altogether.

With the loss of my parents and my husband, I widened my world by joining social groups, volunteering for non-profit organizations, and traveling. With many encounters, ordeals, and adventures, today I have no idea where my box is.

Have you seen my box?

Is That Hearse for Me?

This was the Friday before Memorial Day and the day was nice, no rain, just a comfortable spring day accented with small swarms of gnats. Today would be a great afternoon to visit some of the relatives at the cemetery with floral tributes.

I loaded the car with the flowers, garbage bags, small tool kit, paper towels, hand wipes, and water bottle. I was ready to roll.

One cemetery done with three graves, and I headed back home to get bug spray. Those gnats were hungry.

Pulling into my driveway, I stopped abruptly. There was a big black vehicle parked by the house. It was not a car, not a limo, but a hearse, a black hearse. Why? Was there a memo I hadn't received? Am I checking out? Will I be going to the cemetery in the hearse?

I pulled up alongside the hearse. No one was in the driver's seat and no one was by the house. The sign on the car identified it as Papich-Kuba Funeral Home. I parked my car and went into the house to phone Papich-Kuba. Hearing my voice, Mike Papich immediately started laughing ... for five minutes. He said he knew I would find this funny as well.

He explained the hearse was headed to Des Moines to pick up a "client." The driver thought the car was overheating and didn't want to leave it along the highway. Mike told him to take it to Jeanne Vogt's. Mike just hadn't phoned me. Of course, it was okay. It wasn't in the way of any trucks pulling in or out of the yard.

As I got the bug spray I wondered if any of the neighbors had noticed the hearse and questioned why. Or would they just look in the obituary section of the newspaper for information. Maybe I should check if someone had left food for the bereaved family on the doorstep.

After going to five more cemeteries and fifteen grave sites I returned home expecting to see the hearse still parked there. It was gone!

Once in the house I checked messages. My nephew Darrell had left one. He worked for the towing company. He had been out to pick up the hearse and wondered if I was starting a funeral home. He was sorry he didn't have a camera with him to take a picture.

The next morning Mike Papich called to tell me when he had called the towing service to pick up the hearse, the tow-driver kept saying, "Aunt Jeanne? Aunt Jeanne?" Yes, I am his aunt. And yes, I was glad I was able to drive myself to the cemetery and back home again.

Quilt of Valor

The Quilts of Valor Foundation began in 2003 with a dream, literally a dream. Founder Catherine Roberts' son Nat was deployed in Iraq.

According to the QOV website:

> *The dream was as vivid as real life. I saw a young man sitting on the side of his bed in the middle of the night, hunched over. The permeating feeling was one of utter despair. I could see his war demons clustered around, dragging him down into an emotional gutter. Then, as if viewing a movie, I saw him in the next scene wrapped in a quilt. His whole demeanor changed from one of despair to one of hope and wellbeing. The quilt had made this dramatic change. The message of my dream was: Quilts = Healing.*

I was thrilled to attend an award ceremony presenting the Quilt of Valor to two very deserving veterans on March 15, 2017. Both had served in Vietnam. Both have served as commanders of the same American Legion unit, as well as other positions in their unit, county, and district. They continue to attend and to help at all local Legion events, as well as remodeling the Atkins Legion hall.

On the day of the award ceremony, both men had spent the morning at the Veterans Hospital in Iowa City, side by side receiving their cancer treatments, unaware that the evening would hold a surprise.

There were many family members present that evening, so the men knew this wasn't a normal Legion meeting. Ann Rehbein, Executive Director of the National Quilts of Valor Foundation, made the presentation.

With pride and tears, I wrapped the comforting and healing Quilt of Valor around my oldest son, Ronald Dale Vogt.

Ronald Dale Vogt and David Herman were Quilt of Valor recipients on March 15, 2017.

Standing with the Quilt of Valor, from the left:
Ann Rehbein, Sharon Vogt, Ron Vogt, Bob Rehbein, Jeanne Vogt.

To Tux or Not To Tux

Some people make up their minds to stand firm in their decisions—once made—that's the law. We were days away from our son Tom's wedding ceremony, and the fitting appointments for the men of the wedding party were scheduled.

When tuxedos were the men's attire at other family weddings, my husband Dale would decline the tux saying, "Look I didn't wear a tux when your mother and I got married, and I'm not wearing one now!"

When our son Don got married, Dale said, "Why spend the money on a rental when I can buy a good suit?" It was a medium-blue suit that went nicely with the bridesmaids' gowns and mine. He got years of wear from it.

Now the question was again posed to him. Knowing the answer we all wanted to hear, I reminded him that back home on the farm he wore a tuxedo every day—a high-backed striped OshKosh overall—the farmer's tuxedo, and if he didn't wear a formal tuxedo now, I'd make sure he'd be buried in one.

When he emerged from the fitting room in a white tuxedo, I had never seen him look soooo handsome.

I couldn't keep from looking at my husband in his white tuxedo throughout our son Tom's wedding, reception, dinner, and dance. I'm not sure about the bride and groom's wedding night, but Dale and I had a wonderful one.

Jeanne Krsek Vogt

Haiku by Jeanne

With a haiku, your idea must be expressed within three short lines. The first and the third lines must have exactly five syllables. The second line exactly seven.

Mother's Day is near
If I look in a mirror
She's looking at me!

The red buds of spring
It makes me want to ah-choo
Yes, now spring has sprung

The grass is growing
Flowers are starting to bloom
Sunny days abound

I like ice-cold pop
And coffee starts my mornings
But water is best

September is here
The students are back in school
Class is in session

Thanksgiving is here
Turkey, dressing, many sides
And for dessert ... pie!!

New boots, jewelry, gold
What do you want for Christmas?
Gift cards let you choose

Dolores Anderson Blood

Dolores Anderson Blood was born and raised in Cedar Rapids, Iowa. She married Donald Blood, and raised four daughters: Chris, Cindy, Carol, and Cheri. She has seven grandchildren and five great-grandchildren. Until her retirement in 2005 she worked as a secretary.

For many decades Dolores was active in Campfire and Horizon Clubs. She is a lifelong member of St. Paul's United Methodist Church where she taught Sunday school for about twenty years. She can be found in "her regular pew" on most Sundays. Dolores has volunteered for the National Czech & Slovak Museum & Library for the last twenty-two years, and usually assists in the museum store. She is also a member of The Museum Guild.

Oh, What We Can Learn

Image my surprise when casually reading an article in *The Cedar Rapids Gazette* on June 27, 1999 to learn that the first white man to settle along the Cedar River, where Cedar Rapids is today, was quite possibly James Wilbert Stone, or William, or Billy Stone, as he was also known. And to learn in that same article that he was my great-great-grandfather!

The *Gazette* article stated that Luther Albertus Brewer and Barthinius Larson Wick, for their 1911 book, *The History of Linn County*, had interviewed a Mrs. Elizabeth Hrdlicka, who told them about her father, James Wilbert Stone.

He had been born in Rhode Island and drifted west to Iowa in 1832 or 1833. He followed the Cedar River as far as Ivanhoe, south of Cedar Rapids, where he apparently settled for a time operating a small trading store. Later he came on up the river to the rapids, where he built a cabin, traded with the Indians, and laid out the first "squatter" town. It is said he proposed the town be called Columbus. That was thought to have been in 1837 or 1838.

As I started reading the article, I was a little puzzled, thinking at first it was my grandmother they were talking about having been interviewed, but Grandma was Miss Elizabeth Hrdlicka, not Mrs. Hrdlicka. Then it dawned on me they were talking about her mother, my great-grandmother, who was still living in North Liberty in 1911. I had known that Grandma was named Elizabeth after her mother.

According to Brewer and Wick, a fellow by the name of Osgood Shepherd, who was apparently a scoundrel, a horse thief, and the leader of a band of outlaws, came along afterward and jumped Stone's claim, as one article in Brewer and Wick's book puts it. Not wanting to fight, Billy Stone gave up his claim and moved across the river to the west side, where he continued to trade furs with the Indians.

Robert Ellis, who came to the area later and staked a claim near what is now Ellis Park, stated, "he knew Mr. Stone 'very well', and that he was a 'quiet, congenial, splendid fellow', not a fighting man."

The article stated that "Mr. Stone left the area in 1843, moving to Oxford Township in Johnson County where he married Elizabeth Brown." Two daughters were born to this couple. The first daughter died. Mrs. Stone also passed away four weeks after giving birth to her second daughter, also named Elizabeth. Mr. Stone left his baby daughter with her paternal grandfather, Joseph Brown, who raised her.

Mr. Stone then traveled up the Mississippi River to Hudson, Wisconsin, where he settled. He returned to visit Elizabeth every year, and the last time she talked with him, she said he expressed sorrow that he had "given up his property on the Cedar River, but he hadn't thought then that it would amount to anything." James Wilbert Stone died in Hudson, Wisconsin, at age forty-eight and is buried there.

I was interested to learn from this article that my great-grandfather's middle name was Wilbert. That was my dad's middle name as well as my older brother's. That was not a common name. I had always wondered where their name had come from. I finally found out! Grandma probably would have told me all of these things years ago. Guess I really should have asked more questions when I was young.

Robert S. Chadima

1925 – 2016

Bob was known to say he was a member of the rambunctious Chadima clan in Cedar Rapids. We can't attest to rambunctious, but we do proclaim him a visionary and driving force. The Guild Writers knew Bob as an other-oriented real estate developer who had envisioned what New Bohemia could become, and worked tirelessly to make it happen. He preserved and repurposed three buildings: the Suchy Building, the Kouba Building, and a former factory known as the Cherry Building. The latter provides unique work environments designed to foster the creativity of artists and budding entrepreneurs.

In writing about his youthful work experiences, Bob provides us with a segment of Cedar Rapids history, and some interesting facts about the vanished ice industry.

Melting Assets

Memories of Youth

My family owned the Hubbard Ice Company. Joe Chadima, my granddad had entered the ice business back around 1901 or 1902. I'm not certain how or why. But from then on, his life, and the lives of his extended family, centered on the demands of his company and the ice trade.

As a boy I loved being near the activity and men at the ice house. I watched the blacksmith at his forge— shaping and welding the braces for the ice truck bodies. I helped our carpenter, Jerry Jasa, build the ice truck bodies. I helped place the oak planking as he drove home the screws to bind the boards together. Jerry had few power tools, and his arms were like steel from driving screws home into the oak with an old-fashioned brace.

Jerry's older brother Joe claimed dominion over the ice-cubing machine. I fed the block ice into the crusher and then bagged the crushed ice by size—egg, pea, and snow. I helped Clarence, the truck mechanic, as he replaced bearings and pistons in the truck engines.

In the fall Charlie Cronin dismounted the ice truck body from each truck chassis onto upright barrels in the back lot. I helped. After the ice body was removed from each truck, we then backed a bare truck chassis between barrels on which the oil body had been stored the previous spring. We then tightened the U-bolts that clamped the oil tank to the truck frame, hooked up the power transmission take-off to the pump, and then we were ready for the oil heating season. By changing truck bodies at the end of each heating or ice season, we cut the number of trucks needed by half.

Petey taught me to drive. I had my driving lessons on a twelve-hundred-gallon oil truck. Petey held his arm behind my back, clasping the driver's door handle to brace me as I sat in the driver's seat. That way my feet could reach the gas, brake, and clutch pedals — I felt like a "king of the road" as I drove up Third Avenue. I think I was thirteen or fourteen at the time. Neither Dad nor Grandpa ever found out about Petey's lessons.

Petey also taught me how to listen to the whistle from the customer's oil tank vent. When the whistle pitch increased, I knew to shut off the flow without spilling oil on the lady's flower bed. I'm sure you have heard the same change in pitch as you fill your car's gas tank.

The following summer my job was to ride with each of the drivers in order to catalog each ice route. Cedar Rapids was then a town of about 50,000 people and we ran twenty-seven ice routes. That summer I rode with each driver over his daily route and recorded each stop: where the ice card was hung in the window, where the ice box was, and whether the customer paid cash or had purchased a coupon book. Later on in the year when a driver reported in sick, my route listings became the catalog for the substitute driver.

That was the summer that I learned how to handle ice tongs, how to carry ice without straining my back, how to load the truck so that the ice cakes would neither hit each other and crack, nor lie so close together that the cakes knit together. Often I got to drive the truck. The drivers had their fun with me, too.

I remember a three-story house on J Street Southwest on the top of the hill at Wilson Avenue. The driver told me I could make the delivery. Now I ask you, would you like to carry seventy-five pounds of ice up a hill and three flights of stairs? But I wasn't about to let him know that the boss's kid couldn't do the job.

216

Many of the icemen liked their beer and whiskey. Every so often a driver might stop at a tavern to replenish his liquid levels. Being the boss's son all I got was a Coke. Since the men were paid on the weight of ice they sold they didn't waste time. It was a quick gulp and then back to the truck.

You also sped through your delivery. You would just bang on the screen door, yell "Ice Man," put the ice in the ice box in the kitchen, and pick up the coupon or wait for the lady of the house to bring your twenty-five cents.

I think it was Charlie Cronin that set me up for delivery to a bungalow on Gallagher's Row. That was Fifth Street Northwest.

"Go ahead and take this one, Bobby."

So I banged on the door, yelled "Ice Man," filled the ice box, and waited for my twenty-five cents. Almost immediately a young woman came through the kitchen door wearing nothing but a towel around her waist, but with her twenty-five cents in hand. My sixteen-year-old eyes had never seen such a sight before! At least, not after I was weaned. Charlie laughed for the next two blocks. He knew perfectly well what probably would happen to me at that house, and I'm sure he told the rest of the drivers that evening about Bobby's new experience.

The ice house was a true school to me. Those summers are now fond memories. Those were grand years to be young and to start to learn the ways of the world from the plain but strong working men at the ice house.

In my youth I had no inkling of the history of the ice business I found so exciting. Yet there is an interesting tale to be told about ice as an industry, and about the people who harvested and sold ice right here in Cedar Rapids.

Robert S. Chadima

Early Years of the Domestic Ice Industry

Of course, the easiest method to collect a supply of ice from Mother Nature is to harvest the rivers, ponds, and lakes in northern latitudes. Surely individuals and small cooperative communities must have done so for centuries.

In America the ice industry first thrived in New England. As a community grew, the demand for ice, particularly for food preservation, created opportunity. An enterprising individual might have hopes of earning a profit. Here are some figures from the year 1880 that illustrate both the size of the industry and its importance to the economy:

- There were 1,735 shipments of ice made from Kennebec, Maine, down the Atlantic coast as far south as Charleston, South Carolina, totaling 890,364 tons of ice.
- The ice trade in Maine that year amounted to $1,500,000. Forty percent of that, or $600,000, went to the laborers who harvested, transported, and stored the ice. You can judge the impact of that income by remembering that laborers in Andrew Carnegie's steel mills had an annual wage of $500.
- Along the Hudson River in New York there were 120 ice warehouses between Albany and New York City. These warehouses had a combined storage capacity of 2,866,800 tons of ice. An additional 500,000 tons were piled along the banks of the Hudson for first use in the spring.
- The Hudson valley in 1810, and particularly New York City, consumed over 3,000,000 tons of ice per year.

The domestic ice industry followed the western migration across the northern lands.

Ice and the Export Trade

The foreign ice trade in America was first created by Frederic Tudor of Boston. Yellow fever and malaria were endemic in the American tropics. He sensed that a profit could be earned by shipping ice to the tropics to alleviate the suffering of yellow fever victims. The ice trade turned Tudor into a multimillionaire:

- In 1805 Tudor made the first shipment of ice to the Caribbean.
- In 1807 he sent 240 tons to Havana, Cuba.
- In 1815 the Spanish gave him certain privileges and a monopoly on the ice trade with Havana. After making a delivery to Cuba he wrote in his diary, "Drink, Spaniards and be cool, that I, who have suffered so much in the cause, may be able to go home and keep myself warm."
- In 1833 Tudor sent his first cargo of 200 tons of ice to Calcutta.
- In 1834 he sent his first shipment to Rio de Janeiro.
- By 1837 other Boston entrepreneurs had entered the trade. At that time ice became the largest export trade item from the United States.
- By 1856 there were 363 cargos shipped from the United States consisting of 146,000 tons of ice.

The Ice Industry in Cedar Rapids, Iowa

Before there was an industry, wealthy families sometimes had their own ice storage. The Ely family had their
own private ice supply. They lived during the 1850s in a
white clapboard cottage on the south side of Second Avenue Southeast, between Second and Third streets.

In recalling the family ice pit, John S. Ely wrote:

> The barn was on the alley about forty feet
> from the rear of the house, with a cow shed
> on the west side. The privy and pig pen
> were on the east side of the barn, and ad-
> joining them was the V-shaped vat where
> ashes were stored, later to be leached for
> lye for making soap. Adjoining the leaching
> vat was the ice house, wholly below the
> surface of the ground with only the roof
> showing. In it were stored the blocks of ice
> hauled from the river and covered with
> sawdust for use in the summer. There were
> a number of such ice houses in the village,
> but I recall that ours was in great demand
> in the summer, and its use quite gener-
> ously shared with neighbors. Ice was con-
> sidered a great luxury, there being no pub-
> lic ice house.

Now just stop and think of what Mr. Ely has said:
The ice was packed in sawdust, in a pit in sandy soil, only
a few feet from the barn, the pig pen, the cow shed, and
the privy. *Ice water, anyone?*

Ely had been born in 1853. In his memoir he is remembering his boyhood at the time of our Civil War. Ely's
father was a doctor who served with the Iowa regiment
during the conflict.

We must remember that at this time disease was
thought to be caused by "spontaneous generation." The

genesis of microbiology was only beginning. Semmel-weiss' work in Vienna in the 1840s was controversial, universally ignored, and unheard of in Iowa. Pasteur and Lister were just beginning their work. Bacteria and the germ theory were yet a decade away, even in the medical centers of Europe, much less the backwater of small-town Iowa. As the germ theory of disease became accepted, public sanitation improved. And so did the care with which river ice was harvested, stored, and handled.

Every community that had frozen ponds or rivers found some enterprising individual to harvest and store ice during the wintertime for sale in the summer.

In the village of Cedar Rapids the earliest ice business was that of Elias T. Hooper. He started harvesting ice on the Cedar River, above the dam, after the Civil War.

Charles P. Hubbard arrived in Cedar Rapids in March of 1866 as a twenty-year-old clerk in a leather store. Hubbard's father was a tanner in Oswego, New York, where he had established a leather firm. My guess is that C.P. was sent west to continue the firm in fresh territory. We don't know why C.P. left the leather business; perhaps he sold his interest.

In 1870 Hubbard joined Hooper, and they proclaimed their company as Hooper and Hubbard. Hooper was then thirty-nine and Hubbard was twenty-five.

The Boom Years

Fortuitously it was a great time for Hooper and Hubbard to start their enterprise. In 1870 Cedar Rapids had a population of 6,000 souls.

The decade was a boom time in Cedar Rapids:

- The railroad had arrived in Cedar Rapids the year 1869.
- T.M. Sinclair, who was twenty-nine at the time, was sent to Cedar Rapids by his family in Ireland to found a hog packing plant in 1871.
- Robert Stuart and his father migrated to Cedar Rapids from Ontario to found the North Star Oatmeal Mill, 1873 (now Quaker Oats).

These new plants created an increased demand for labor in the small village. They also made opportunities for supportive businesses by enterprising individuals. The population of the town more than doubled during that decade. Hooper and Hubbard had luckily timed their startup company at the beginning of the boom.

Hubbard was an aggressive young man, as well as astute, and clever. You can imagine him as a brash young man about town, who made it his business to know all the important people of the small community. I assume that he had a greater amount of capital than Hooper, possibly from the sale of his leather business.

In 1882 after twelve years of joint operation, Hubbard acquired Hooper's interest in the firm. It may be that Hubbard sensed a future conflict with Hooper's son Walter and felt that it could best be resolved by separation of their interests sooner rather than later. From then on Hubbard dominated the ice business in Cedar Rapids.

Ice was so vitally important to our community that the ice trade nearly assumed the status of a public utility. *The Gazette* reported in 1886 that "The weather remains cold and the ice harvest is great. It is a boon for poor working men and it is plain that an ice crop is about as essential as a corn crop. About $8,000 was paid out last week by ice companies to men for their work and for their

teams, and this money is all spent in Cedar Rapids."
(1/21/1886)

Nearly every year *The Gazette* reported the quality
of the ice being harvested and forecast the next summer's
price to the housewife. If there were a poor ice harvest it
was a distress for the entire community; a failed harvest
was a calamity for all.

Hubbard advertised regularly in *The Gazette*. In
later years, as public health standards and awareness
had become important, Hubbard hired a pathologist from
the University of Iowa to test a sample of his ice from the
river each year, and grandly announced the pathologist's
report to *The Gazette's* readers. He didn't mention that
one ten-pound sample might not be representative of a
fifteen-thousand-ton harvest. Hubbard also kept the public informed of the care with which the slush, snow, and
dirt were scraped from the ice as it was harvested.

After 1915, Hubbard owned an artificial ice plant,
while his competitors, including my granddad Chadima,
were still harvesting all their ice from the river. Hubbard
changed his story to emphasize that his ice had not been
harvested by men spitting tobacco juice on the ice, nor by
horses working over the ice as it was harvested.

Hubbard acquired harvesting rights in other communities: Shell Rock, Rockport, and as far away as Spirit Lake. He always had that northern ice as back up in case of a weak crop here on the Cedar River. He shipped the ice from those points south to Missouri, even as far as New Mexico.

During a particularly bad harvest Hubbard bought ice from points as far north as St. Paul and had it shipped to Cedar Rapids. Hubbard's energetic enterprise as well as his capital resources always kept the Hubbard Ice Company ahead of all his competitors. At various times other men entered and then left the business.

During the winter of 1882-1883 Hubbard harvested 15,180 tons of ice:

- 8,000 tons in his own ice houses
- 3,000 tons Eagle Brewery
- 1,300 tons Williams brewery
- 400 tons Walker & Passmore egg
- 1,000 tons Morin Company, creamery and egg
- 600 tons Elmer Higley egg
- 400 tons Chicago Northwestern RR
- 180 tons Chicago, Milwaukie, & St. Paul RR
- 300 tons for individual consumers

The meat packing company T. M. Sinclair had their own ice operation. They harvested 24,000 tons of ice on the west side of the river and 45,000 tons of ice on the east side of the river.

Over the next thirty years a number of firms competed for the growing ice market. Besides Hooper and Hubbard, there were John Huggins, Taylor and Davis, J. R. Mann, T. E. Sleight, and my family, the Chadima Brothers.

The Gazette stories reported that over ten days to two weeks, some 650 men were needed for the ice harvest. Men were paid $1.00 per day and a man with a team

$1.50. There were no electric saws or gasoline engines. The entire harvest was made by muscle power—scoring the ice in the river, breaking it free, floating it to the take-out chute, pulling it to the ice house, and hauling it up ramps to be layered into place in the ice houses.

The harvest was not without its dangers. This story is from the *Gazette* of January 12, 1894:

> Many curious sights are seen on the river.
> A too-adventurous horse slips into the river off the glossy ice. Three or four men rush to him and the moment his head comes up, a noose is thrown over it onto his neck, and he is choked. Oddly enough this causes his body to be inflated. He is pulled to the edge of the ice and a plank slipped under him; everybody pulls away and presto! He stands on solid ice shaking himself in a moment.

My granddad told me he never lost a horse on the river. If a horse did break through the ice Granddad would pull him back on the ice, pour a quart of whiskey into him, then run the horse to Ellis Park and back before returning him to his barn stall.

In February 1906, John Pollock, who was working at the Sinclair ice harvest was not so lucky. He lost his team of horses when they broke through the ice into twelve feet of water. The *Gazette* reported:

> The team was worth about two hundred and fifty dollars, and the loss will prove a severe one to Mr. Pollock, as he is a man well along in years and the horses were his only means of support.

The Beginning of the End

Ice had been made artificially as early as the 1850s. As latitude decreases, the demand for cooling is steadily more urgent. Even before electricity became prevalent there were artificial ice plants in the south. They were experimental, dangerous, and inefficient, but those experimental contraptions were harbingers of the machines yet to come.

It was the arrival of the electric utility that made artificial ice a commercial reality. The Sinclair Packing plant installed the first artificial plant in Cedar Rapids at the turn of the twentieth century. C. P. Hubbard followed Sinclair's lead by building his block ice plant within the next decade. Hubbard's artificial plant could manufacture sixty tons per day which was not enough to meet the annual demand for our community, so ice continued to be harvested from the river.

The winter of 1921-1922 saw a failure of the ice harvest on the river. My grandfather, who had only the river as a source of ice, suffered a nervous breakdown as a result of the ice failure. I'm sure that it was as a result of the harvest failure that the following summer Chadima Brothers and Hubbard merged into a single company.

By 1929 it was obvious that the split ownership would no longer work. My grandfather and his four sons then bought out the interest of the other owners. They kept the historic name, Hubbard Ice and Fuel. Granddad signed the purchase agreement, specifying payment in gold two weeks before the stock market collapsed on Black Thursday in October of 1929.

When my poor granddad confronted the economic crash of 1929, he did not have the lucky timing that Hooper & Hubbard had enjoyed fifty-nine years earlier when in 1870 they sailed into Cedar Rapids' greatest boom. Nonetheless Granddad with his four sons paid off their debt within five years.

Holding On

Our family's last harvest from the river was made in the winter of 1929. In 1936 we built a new 100 ton-per-day ice plant. That plant was one of the last block ice plants built in this country. In my teens did I know that those days were just about the top of the ice industry's prosperity?

The inroads upon the ice industry made by electric refrigeration stopped when our country entered World War II. There were no raw materials to manufacture refrigeration units. Those materials were needed for the war effort. The country had to rely upon block ice.

The military draft took the men, and so during the war, ice delivery in the hot months of summer came to depend on high school boys.

Until I joined the Navy in 1943, I worked at the ice house from the time school was out in May until it started again in September. My younger brothers followed me and brought some of their friends along. Fifteen- and sixteen-year-old boys had great fun at the work.

My brother Bill and his friends confessed that one of their favorite stunts was to throw the truck, loaded with three tons of ice, out of gear at the top of the hill on Mount Vernon road to see how fast they could go by the time they reached the bottom.

After the War, our twenty-seven ice routes had shrunk to two. The electric refrigerator took our business away from us. My poor mother, I think, was just about the last wife in Cedar Rapids to get an electric refrigerator. That was in 1954.

When I left the Navy in 1956 I found that the ice business was still great fun. We survived by making a number of changes. We expanded our markets. We made our own vending stations and were able to place them in many small towns in eastern Iowa. We delivered ice to our stations as far east as Clinton and as far south as Washington.

We supplied all the cooling for the meat packing plant in Postville, a hundred miles north of Cedar Rapids. When urban renewal took out the ice plant in Des Moines, we delivered semi-loads to their local ice man. We learned one lesson the hard way about delivering ice over long distances. An overweight fine could easily be more than the load of ice was worth.

We found unusual uses for ice. The atomic plant at Palo, for instance, used huge amounts of ice. It was mixed into the concrete in order to speed its curing.

Perhaps you have noticed the lion statues at the entry to the Masonic Library. They provided another unusual use of ice. Those stone lions weighed tons and were difficult to handle. When it came time to put the lions in place, each statue was placed on blocks of ice. Then they could be guided into position slowly and easily as the ice melted from under them.

On stifling summer days, the Paramount Theater was cooled by fans blowing air over Hubbard ice and into air vents to cool the theater patrons.

We also sought efficiencies. By using spare freezer space, we were able to manufacture pallet loads of crushed and cubed ice during the winter for next summer's delivery.

We also helped other companies to become more efficient. It was the cold storage business that saved our ice business. We could manufacture ice at very little cost as an adjunct to cold storage freezers.

I was able to automate our own refrigeration plant for increased efficiency. In case of failure, the pressure, temperature, and vibration sensors on the equipment could shut down the compressors faster than men could. That meant we no longer needed an engineer on duty twenty-four hours a day to oversee the compressors and to pull ice during the night. We were able to run a normal forty-hour work week.

Over time, it became more and more difficult to find efficiencies. At the same time smaller and smaller machines made it easy for the supermarkets and other ice users to manufacture their own ice supply. Today, of course, most every refrigerator has its own ice maker.

Letting Go

I left the ice business to my cousins in 1965. Since then it has faded away to practically nothing. I miss those exciting times in the ice business that I enjoyed in those youthful boy and teen years. They are long gone, never to come again. That wonderful ice business will not be revived by nostalgia. I am left with only a great store of frozen memories of those days at the ice house.

Bibliography:

The Ice Industry of the United States, Henry Hall, Census Division U. S. Department of the Interior, 1880

Cedar Rapids Gazette, microfilm files, Cedar Rapids Public Library.

Tales of the Town, Ralph Clemons

The New Yorker, February 12, 2001

Popular Science Monthly, vol VOCII, March 1888

The Nation, November 29, 1900

History of Linn County, George Henry

The Illustrated Review, Cedar Rapids, Iowa, 1900

The Biographical Review of Linn County, S. J. Clarke, Chicago, 1900

Coda

Bob Chadima passed on before writing a memoir about the Chadima Ice Wagons and the Stone City Summer Art Colony. This coda has been written in Bob's honor.

Gypsy Caravan

Bob was a rambunctious seven-year-old in 1932. Our country was in the third year of the great depression. His grandfather, Joseph Chadima, was still struggling to honor his contract to purchase the Hubbard Ice company. Bob has written, *"Granddad signed the purchase agreement, specifying payment in gold two weeks before the stock market collapsed on Black Thursday in October of 1929."* Money was tight.

It was in this difficult financial environment that Joe Chadima received a visit from artist Grant Wood, who was promoting an innovative idea for a summer art colony to help train young Midwest artists. Many might not have considered an arts colony a high priority during a depression, but Chadima knew of Wood's reputation and was willing to listen.

A couple of years before, Wood had received instant fame as the winner of the Norman Wait Harris Medal in a competition at the Art Institute of Chicago. He had entered two paintings: *Stone City* and *American Gothic*. The third prize Harris Medal carried with it a $300 prize and was awarded to *American Gothic*. The museum then purchased that painting for an additional $300. His *Stone City* painting was not accepted into the competition and was returned to the artist.

However, it is that *Stone City* painting that was the impetus for Wood calling upon Chadima. He had painted it in 1930. According to Wanda M. Corn, who wrote the definitive book, *Grant Wood the Regionalist Vision:*

> The *Stone City* painting was "the first work that Wood completely painted in his new style. His decorative geometries ... he now applied with a gleeful abandon, riotously reducing everything to a rounded or rectilinear shape, sweeping surfaces clean of irregularities, and inventing a profusion of different patterns of trees and fields ... It set a style the artist would refine and modify, but never fundamentally alter, the rest of his life."

Wood had fallen in love with the hillside where he had set up his easel to paint *Stone City*. He began to dream of creating a summer artist's colony. There was a magnificent hard limestone mansion on the property that had been built in 1883 by John A. Green, the owner of the nearby quarry. During the eighteen-hundreds, the hard limestone in the quarry had been cut to construct large buildings and bridges across our country. However, with the advent of Portland Cement in the late eighteen-hundreds, the hard limestone industry declined.

The mansion had been abandoned for thirty years by the time Wood began to paint his picture on the hillside above the Wapsipinicon River. What others may have seen as a dilapidated building, Grant Wood saw as the nucleus for an arts community.

In the midst of the depression, while still riding high from the success of *American Gothic,* Wood and two friends, Ed Rowan and Adrian Dornbush, decided to establish their innovative summer arts colony. With neither financial backing, nor business acumen, they moved forward.

They turned the mansion into a dormitory. The basement contained the plumbing and showers. The first floor provided a living room, dining room, and kitchen. The second floor had sleeping quarters for the women. The attic had sleeping quarters for the men.

An ice house on the property was transformed into an artists' gallery, and a rathskeller, called *The Sickle & Sheaf*.

The trio visited small towns across the state with the goal of recruiting thirty students. They were surprised by receiving ninety-two requests from young artists wanting to spend their summer in Stone City. In addition, fifteen students were driven daily from Cedar Rapids for morning art classes.

With so many applicants, additional housing was urgently needed. In the book, *My Brother, Grant Wood,* Nan Wood Graham recalls that as a youth "Grant had an unfulfilled dream to buy an old ice wagon, and a horse, and to take long leisurely sketching trips along back-roads with Mother and me." Now, decades later Grant was envisioning transforming ice wagons into living space for his male faculty.

Thus, he appeared on Joe Chadima's doorstep in the hopes that Hubbard Ice could provide ice wagons they were no longer using. Joe provided Grant with fourteen ice wagons. In exchange, Wood agreed to offer a scholarship to a talented high school art student.

Grants sister remembered:

> Grant got official permission to tow the ice wagons to Stone City at 4 a.m., when the highway was least busy. The wooden wheels were covered with iron bands, and the old wagons protested the move with great clatter and rattling—both on paving and dirt roads.

Previously, the faculty had agreed to teach for six weeks without salary. They now accepted, with good humor, the fact that they would also be living in primitive ice wagons.

Photographer: John W. Barry, Jr.

Kaleidoscope

Grant Wood painting his ice wagon

Ed Rowan relaxing on his ice wagon

Photographer: John W. Barry, Jr.

They built a lower, and upper, folding bunk into each wagon. The entrances and window-like areas were screened, maintaining the lovely views and cool prairie breezes, while keeping out the mosquitoes. The wagons were furnished with hand-me-downs. The men then set to work to see who could decorate their wagon in the most interesting manner. They opened the summer art colony to the general public for Saturday night dances, charging forty cents. On Sundays, ten cents would admit a curiosity seeker.to the grounds. Between five hundred and a thousand people might come on a weekend. A few purchased art from the gallery. More bought the chicken dinners in the dining room, or snacks in the rathskeller. All marveled at the fantastic ice wagons—including reporters from the east coast, west coast, and points in between.

We believe Bob Chadima's grandfather most assuredly would have taken his grandson to visit that encamped on the hillside above the Wapsipinicon, as the manner in which his ice wagons had been so imaginatively repurposed was receiving national and international press. We can only imagine his excitement.

The romance of the ice wagons still brings summer visitors to Stone City each summer to view replicas of the Hubbard Ice wagons. The brightly painted gypsy caravan is the enduring symbol for Grant Wood's innovative art venture. The Chadima family, to this day, continues to enable artists and help build community.

Gypsy Caravan text © 2018 Sandra Cermak Hudson

References

Wanda M. Corn, *Grant Wood: The Regionalist Vision*, Yale University Press, 1983, p. 74

Nan Wood Graham, *My Brother, Grant Wood*, State Historical Society of Iowa, 1993, Chapter 9.

Photographer: John W. Barry, Jr.
Stone City Art Colony Painting Class, ca. 1932-33.
Back row: Marvin Cone (at easel) and Adrian Dornbush.

Photographer: John W. Barry, Jr.
John Steuart Curry and Grant Wood at the Stone City Art Colony 1933

Joseph Kurka

Joseph Kurka is a full-blood Czech. He was born and raised in Phillips, Wisconsin, and served in World War II. He married Mardella Lala and is the father of twins, Jeff and Kathy, and a son David. Joe has six grandchildren and one great-granddaughter. He had a career as a mechanical technologist (model maker) and is retired from the Square D Company. For fifty years Joe was a very active member of Jan Hus Presbyterian Church before joining St. Paul's United Methodist Church about ten years ago. Joe is an active member and Past Master of Crescent Masonic Lodge, and sits on the Advisory Board of The Scottish Rights. Joe has recently retired from serving twenty-two years as volunteer for the National Czech & Slovak Museum & Library.

Over The Bounding Waves!

In the early 1940s, during World War II, there was an uneasy feeling for young men as to whether they should enlist in the Armed Services or wait to be drafted. I chose to wait.

After graduating from high school, I went to Chicago where my older brother was working. There was more work to be had than in my small home town of Phillips, Wisconsin. After about a year working in a defense plant making airplane generators, I was drafted for service in the U. S. Navy where men were needed at that time.

I had practically grown up on the water. My grandparents lived on the "flowage," and my father had built a boat that was kept at the dock in their backyard. I spent a good share of my time boating, fishing, or swimming, yet I did not want to be in the navy, so I requested army duty. They were very reluctant about it, but finally agreed.

I was sent to Vancouver, Washington for basic training. Part of my training included a period of maneuvers in Bend, Oregon. I was assigned, along with two other men, to one small pup tent. It was hot during the daytime and cold at night. The ground was so hard it was uncomfortable for sleeping. We found a haystack in a field nearby and swiped some hay to put on the ground to make sleeping a little more comfortable. After six weeks of basic training we were sent by truck to Camp Haan in Riverside, California for additional training.

March Air Force Base was just across the highway from Camp Haan. I had always been interested in flying. My buddy, John Mossburger, and I decided to try for a transfer to the Air Force. We took the tests and passed, but later I received a call informing me I couldn't transfer because of a defective valve in my heart. They said it probably wouldn't affect my normal life, but they couldn't take a chance at high altitudes. I had to stay in the army, while my buddy, John, went into the air force without me.

Shortly afterwards, my unit was sent to Camp Stoneman, California, where we prepared to go overseas. We boarded the *Noordam,* which was a passenger liner that had been converted into a troop carrier, and sailed for a month with no idea where we were going.

The ocean was very rough most days with lots of storms. I spent a good share of the month being "sick as a dog"! I had been assigned to duty in the galley, but after the first day when they realized how sick I was, they told me, "get out of here—as sick as you are—we don't need you." So I lost my job!

I spent most of the time lying on the deck of the ship, if it wasn't raining, or on my cot in the hold, or *hanging over the rail!*

One night my buddies wanted me to see how bad the storm was and how high the waves were. They helped me up to the deck and leaned me against the bulkhead. They held me up so I wouldn't fall over. The bow of the ship was pitching up and down with the waves rolling over the deck. After watching for a bit, they took me back to the hold, soaking wet from the waves. To this day, I can picture those waves and the ship pitching up and down!

During that month on the ocean, we had to use salt water for our showers. That was quite a challenge, as the soap wouldn't even work up a lather. It was almost useless to even try. We simply went without showering until we reached our destination. We certainly needed showers by that time!

Eventually we reached an island and could see that the tops of the trees had all been shot up or blown off from the artillery shells. The beach was littered with tanks and equipment that had been destroyed and left abandoned. Sharks were swimming around in the water nearby. That was when they informed us we were in New Guinea. It would be our home for the next two years.

We and our equipment were taken ashore in amphibious ducks. We walked along a dirt road to a clearing in the middle of the jungle and proceeded to set up a base. Our tents consisted of a canvas canopy over a wooden platform. No walls. We slept under mosquito netting.

Our unit was a supply/maintenance unit. It was our job to supply and repair equipment for the combat units who were fighting the nearby Japanese army.

The first night they wanted men to patrol the camp area for security purposes, and wouldn't you know, I was chosen. It was complete darkness. We weren't even allowed to light a cigarette! That was a little scary, not knowing anything about the area or just where the Japs were. Sometimes we could hear them in the jungle, but of course we couldn't see them.

Later we found out the Japs were stealing our ammunition. I wondered why, since the type of ammunition they were taking didn't fit the Japanese equipment. Then one time we were exploring a part of the jungle nearby and came across a Japanese pillbox. We found and recovered some of the equipment that had been stolen. Shortly after, a Japanese soldier appeared on the road we had just been on and we captured him.

My main job was doling out supplies. Sometimes I helped load gasoline tanks onto C-47 planes at a nearby airstrip. When we were there overnight, we slept on top of those gasoline tanks! You have to wonder about some of our choices!

The New Guinea natives lived throughout the jungle in shacks built on stilts. They liked the Americans and sometimes would come into our camp with seashells they had collected. Some of the men would purchase them as souvenirs, paying for them with extra cigarettes they had been given.

Occasionally, we would wake up in the middle of the night to find a native standing in our tent! They never bothered us. They just stood there. What did bother us was hearing rats scampering around in the tent. They were looking for crackers and/or cheese that someone might have left out. We had to keep everything like that, along with our clothing, in our foot lockers.

One day an officer gave us a large netting. It was about five feet by thirty feet. We tied one end to a jeep, then swam out into the ocean with the other end to see if we could catch some fish—but caught a shark instead. When the officer saw what we pulled in, he said, "no more." We had to give up our net.

Hearing there was a native village in the vicinity, we wanted to see it. We were allowed to go, but had to have an Australian soldier with us. We drove a truck to where the road ended, then hiked several more miles. The village consisted of a small number of shacks on stilts built close together. They were not scattered throughout the jungle like most natives lived. They treated us very well, and loaded us up with piles of bananas to take back to the base. We were informed there was fighting taking place not too far away, but the Japs never bothered the natives.

After being in New Guinea for two years, our enlistment was over, and it was time to come back to the United States. Trucks took us to the dock where we found Japanese prisoners loading the ship with tires that had been salvaged from trucks and jeeps. We had to wait until that was finished before we were allowed on the beach to begin boarding the troop ship. I was a little apprehensive about another month on the ocean, but it wasn't nearly as stormy. The seas were calmer, so I didn't experience seasickness, except during periods of rough weather.

Upon arriving in the USA, we were sent to Camp McCoy in Sparta, Wisconsin to be discharged.

Home again! I was very glad to be home, but will never forget my experiences in New Guinea, more than seven decades ago!

Produced by -
Bill Floryancic

Marjorie Kopecek Nejdl

Marj is a second-generation Czech-American. She has been designated a Master Czech Folk Artist by the Iowa Arts Council, and has demonstrated and taught her art form across our state and nation. The kaleidoscope on the cover of this book is a gift from Marj to our Guild Writers. We are honored. Marj was a charter member of our group, but resigned when she found it was taking her away from her folk art, which is her life passion. She has agreed, however, to share four short stories that she wrote when she was an active member. Our group wrote the coda entitled *Our Marj,* and included pictures to give you an idea of her creativity.

First Endeavor
February 13, 2014

Well, I can't believe I am enrolling in this "memoir writers" group. Words, that is, descriptive words, don't come easy for me. So here I am. I guess I'll start with an early memory.

I can't attest that this is a memory, or if I remember it being told to me. However, my assumption is that I was around three years old. My mother just finished painting the screened-in porch and was out in the backyard talking with my grandmother. Evidently, the clouds were forming, and the conversation went to "vypadat ze bude pršet," looks like rain. With those words, I made a mad dash across the newly-painted porch, leaving gray footprints throughout the house. Needless to say, I did end up with a spanking. Can't remember if it rained or not.

Translation: I want a hug

An Egg Artist? Really?

I was raised in a household where a wealth of Czech culture prevailed. My father, born in Czechoslovakia, came to the United States as a young boy. My mother was born in Cedar Rapids, Iowa, of Czech heritage.

After my maternal grandmother's death, my mother traveled to Czechoslovakia with her father. She was about four years old. She returned to Cedar Rapids before her eighteenth birthday.

In our home, we spoke the Czech language. I was fortunate to grow up surrounded by Czech folk art treasures. As a young girl, I learned the art of old-world Czech egg decorating known as *kráslice* from my uncle Martin Polehna. He lived next door. Every Easter he would prepare the dyes to decorate eggs. My cousin Vera, Uncle Martin, and I worked together enjoying the art and the comradeship.

In 1972 a Czech festival was organized in Cedar Rapids. My uncle Martin was to demonstrate the art of *kráslice*. His health, however, began to fail, and he told the organizers that I would do the demonstration. He just forgot to tell me.

A phone call came to give me dates and times. Dates and times? For what? I was told I would be giving the demonstration of the *batik* method of *kráslice*. What? I was a little upset, as I would need to get the materials together, get organized to do this project, and try to fit it into our family's schedules.

It all worked out, and I am so thankful to Uncle Martin, and the organizers of the Czech festival. Since then I have concentrated on Czech folk art. It has been my life's work. In 1986, I was honored to receive the title of *Master Czech Folk Artist* from the Iowa Arts Council.

Through my art I have tried to promote and preserve Czech folk art, teaching in many states. I had an exciting two weeks on the Washington, DC, Mall, displaying and instructing for the Smithsonian Sesquicentennial Celebration in 1996. I have also

been fortunate to be commissioned by the National Czech & Slovak Museum & Library, to paint eggs for many dignitaries.

It's been fun, and the icing on the cake is that my grandchildren, the next Czech generation, are now helping with my classes
at the museum. What fun!

Examples of Marj Nejdl's kráslice eggs

Above: an example of a *kráslice* egg.

Top right opposite: Marj and granddaughter Emily Nejdl as a child.

Bottom right opposite: Marj is on the right leaning forward, her granddaughter Emily is on her left, and her grandson Tom is on Marj's right.

First Day in Art School
September 1955

Well, I survived the first week in Chicago. Discovered a few interesting things about our neighborhood. My mother worried about our dingy dorm room—huh—if she only knew! A block west of us was a famous area named Rush Street, with restaurants and bars frequented by the Chicago gangsters, as we were told.

The first day of school was finally here. My roommate Betty and I walked the five blocks south to our school thinking we were big shots, walking at a brisk pace with the crowd. Chicago people are fast pacers. When we reached the school office, they sent me to my class on the 6th floor. With my art pad under my arm and my toolbox in my other hand, I pressed the elevator button.

As I entered the classroom, there were about five or six men students sitting astride their art easel seats. As I turned the corner—whoa, *good lord*!! They sent me to the wrong class. There sat a *big, black, nude man*.

I couldn't turn around fast enough to get back to the elevator to punch the down button. For heaven's sake, that elevator is taking its sweet time. Should I take the stairs? This was a lot to take in for this naïve high school girl from Iowa. By that time the elevator door opened and I rushed in to literally *punch* the down button! I marched into the office and complained they had sent me to the wrong class.

No, Marjorie Kopecek.

Monday morning.

Life Drawing, 6th floor.

Well, now what do I do? Go back to the probably-snickering class with the nude, or skip class and go back to the dorm? I figured I might as well go back upstairs and face the music. The instructor checked me in. The guys, I could see, were trying to conceal their grins. I found a saw horse, as I called them, and settled in. Egads, where do I start?! The instructor came over, sat next to me, told me how to get started, and made me feel that I would be part of the class.

Gradually, you stop thinking of the models as nudes, but rather as anatomies to learn the proper proportions and placement. Most models were students earning extra money. Thank goodness I didn't need the extra money.

That was the start of a fun and productive education. My parents did get the information about all of the incidents at school and in the neighborhoods, when I felt it safe to deal them out.

A Giant Birthday Party

Both the State of Iowa and the Smithsonian Institution celebrated their 150th birthday in July 1996. And what celebrations they were!

It all started in the fall of 1995. A representative from the Smithsonian came to our home to interview me concerning my Czech folk art—mainly my decorated eggs. My husband Ed was in the kitchen baking strudel for our church harvest festival. So, our guest also got to sample the strudel and talk with Ed.

After a year of researching every corner of the state and interviewing over seven hundred people, the Smithsonian was ready to reveal the names of the Iowans who would represent the state at the two-week-long Festival of American Folklife that would take place on the National Mall in Washington, DC.

The word came to us by a phone call on April 1st. Ed wasn't at home, so I left him a note, as I had an egg demonstration. When I returned, I was disappointed that he wasn't very excited. The note I had left him read, "Pack your bags, you're going to Washington, DC, to make strudel!" The reason for his unconcern—he thought it was an April Fools' joke.

The next two months proved to be *very* busy. Easter with egg orders, preparation for our son's wedding, and then the big trip for the celebration on the National Mall.

After arriving in Washington, DC, we unpacked and attended the orientation. Our festival site preparation went smoothly, and we were soon ready to do "our thing" for two weeks.

The presentations wouldn't go into operation for two days, so we had a couple of evenings to see the sights. The first night out we went to the Vietnam Memorial

Monument. Very impressive. Ed had a new partial denture inserted the week before, and it now was giving him a problem. So, to spend the evening without pain, he removed it and put it in his pocket. We spent the next hour and a half viewing and enjoying the sights.

Soon it was time to return to the hotel, so we hailed a cab and headed back. Ed paid the driver and we went upstairs. When we entered our room, he emptied his pockets—oh—oh, his partial denture was missing! It must have fallen out of his pocket when he paid for the cab ride. He rushed downstairs, outside, to look for it, but nowhere, nothing to be found!

"Oh great! Now what are you going to do?" I was a little perturbed to say the least! Giving his presentation, he would have a big gap showing.

"This is really going to look good—the old bohemie without a couple of teeth!" Now what!

Well, you know they say that George Washington had wooden teeth, so Ed Nejdl is going to have wax teeth. I took some of my beeswax from the egg decorating supplies and formed two side teeth. Perfect! Naturally, he couldn't eat with them, but they certainly looked good just talking, if I do have to say so myself.

The festival was divided into three parts: *Iowa Community Style, The American South, and Working at the Smithsonian.* We were part of a rather large Iowa contingent. There were representatives from all walks of life. A sample of the occupational traditions included a towboat captain, a boatbuilder, a commercial fisherman, an auctioneer, a farmer, a tool and die maker, a volunteer fireman, and a news reporter.

Among the artistic traditions was my Czech folk art, Danish and Swedish handwork quilters, a Meskwaki bead worker, a quinceanera doll maker, a wood carver, a scrollsaw clock maker, and a tinsmith.

Ed's strudel making was part of the foodway traditions that included ethnic cooks and bakers, and even butchers and meat locker operations.

The performance traditions included not only bands, vocalists, instrumentalists, and a square dance caller, but also a girls' basketball team.

Our jobs were to showcase our specialties, visit with the people about Iowa, and let them learn about us and our communities. I felt that Ed and I were good ambassadors for Cedar Rapids, our National Czech & Slovak Museum & Library, and our ethnic community in general.

Ed's schedule lasted about two hours a day. When he finished his job, he came over and helped me, as my schedule was for the whole day. Besides talking and demonstrating, I had a children's class each day for one hour that turned out to be fun for the kids and the Smithsonian volunteer helpers.

The festival had over 1,299,000 visitors with 500,000 people on the 4th of July alone. On that day, one gate keeper had 28,000 visitors come through in two hours. Our son and daughter-in-law, Chuck and DeeAnn, stayed on that evening for the fireworks display.

Over those two weeks we talked with many people eager to know about Iowa. We also met people with Iowa connections. There were those who knew us, and those who knew so-and-so, or were former neighbors of neighbors, and so the hours passed. The Czech and Slovaks from the eastern United States were surprised to learn about the Czechs in the Midwest. We met a lot of pleasant people, and so many nice things happened for us, too many to mention. We had a grand and memorable time, felt we did a good job, and were looking forward to doing it all over again for the Iowa Folk Festival and the 150th birthday celebration on the grounds of the State Capitol Building in Des Moines.

The Smithsonian staff and our Iowa committee people were great. Their graciousness made our job a little easier. We just want to say to Iowa and the Smithsonian Institution—Thank You!

Marj and Ed Nejdl

Kaleidoscope

Marj with artist Catharine Otto

The photograph is from the intermedia art project "Stezky/Pathways" by artist Sonya Darrow (pictured here with Marj Nejdl). Sonya created a ritual around Marj's hugs: "A hug from Marj Nejdl is like getting a hug from Czech culture itself / Objetí od Marj Nejdlje jako by vás objala česká kultura samotná." It is part of the artist's practice to honor the "Keepers of Tradition" in each of Iowa's Czech settlements.

Marjorie Kopecek Nejdl

Multiple authors have written the story that follows. As a group we spent a stimulating morning interviewing Marj Nejdl. We then each wrote our own article about Marj before again coming together to select a paragraph from one story and a sentence from another to create our single "group write" which we call Our Marj. It was a fun and challenging process.

Our Marj

Every visitor to the National Czech & Slovak Museum & Library has likely experienced the art of Marjorie Kopecek Nejdl. She has gifted her talents to foster the success of the museum from its earliest days.

In the 1970s she was among a small group of second and third generation Czech Americans to form the Czech Fine Arts Foundation. That group opened a small museum in a three-room house on C Street SW, just south of 16th Avenue—colloquially it is *The Avenue.* In Marj's childhood, it was the major Czech shopping area.

As the Foundation's acquisitions grew, so did its aspirations. In less than twenty years the small committee became a national organization with an impressive new facility. It was built on a plot of land next to the Cedar River between 14th and 16th Avenues SW.

Just like Marj, that organization is vibrant, energetic, and resilient. This was never more evident than after the unprecedented 2008 flood of the Cedar River. The flood waters devastated the building and its collections. The response was to come back bigger and better. The entire museum was jacked-up, rotated, moved to higher ground, and enlarged.

Marj was there in the beginning, and now four decades later, she still actively promotes Czech heritage. She literally has dedicated thousands of volunteer hours in support of the museum.

She is a respected and sought-after mentor who is passionate in sharing her skills, and teaching others the artistry and science of creating Czech folk art.

The museum gift shop has sold Marj's Czech signs, decorated eggs, shirts, aprons, pottery, refrigerator magnets, and books with her designs on their covers and containing articles and photographs of her art.

Translation: Shop until you drop

In the two months before Christmas Marj spends many hours in the museum gift shop where she personalizes customers' purchases of Christmas tree ornaments by applying calligraphy and folk art. As she works, she enjoys talking with her guests, hearing their stories, and joyously sharing her own Czech memories.

Marj also designs announcements, posters, placemats, napkins, and more for special events like *The Taste of Czech and Slovak,* and the *Sweetheart Dinners.*

Presidents Kovac, Clinton, & Havel at the dedication of the new National Czech & Slovak Museum & Library. Marj Nejdl's logo for the museum is on the wall of the building.

Marjorie Kopecek Nejdl

Presidents Clinton, Havel, and Kovac

This story concerns the visit to Cedar Rapids by United States President Bill Clinton, Czech President Vaclav Havel, and Slovakian President Michal Kovac in October 1995. They came for the dedication of the National Czech & Slovak Museum & Library.

With less than three weeks before the big day, Marj was asked to create commemorative gifts for the three presidents: specifically, three souvenir *kráslice* goose eggs, intricately-painted with Czech folk art and the museum's new logo. Marj was honored, yet three weeks was a short timeframe for designing and painting one egg, let alone three.

She had barely managed to get her supplies together, when she received a phone call. The timeframe suddenly shrank by several days. Marj was informed the Federal Bureau of Investigation would need the eggs five days before the event. The eggs would have to be put through their forensic laboratory to ensure there was nothing concealed within. That phone call necessitated burning some midnight oil, but all ended well. In fact, better than just well. Marj, as a Czech speaker, was invited to present President Havel with his egg.

In telling this story, Marj laughs as she recalls that when she entered elementary school her primary language was Czech, yet she spoke enough English to be the interpreter for four boys who spoke only Czech. Today English flows off of her tongue like music.

On that sunny October day as she presented her egg to President Vaclav Havel, she was thankful that her parents had gifted her their Czech language.

Astronaut Eugene Cernan

This story is about Astronaut Eugene Cernan, who was of Czech heritage. In 1972 he flew the Apollo 17 mission, which made him the last man to walk on the moon.

That mission was Cernan's third trip to outer space. Earlier he had been the second man to walk in space, and he had also previously walked on the moon. It was on this final moon trip that the Apollo crew captured the iconic blue marble image of earth. It was fun to learn that before returning to earth Cernan had left his daughter's initials in the lunar dust.

When in 1997 Marj was asked to design and decorate an egg for Cernan, she must have felt a thrill of *to the moon and back.* Sorry, we couldn't resist.

When Eugene Cernan returned to the museum in 2015 to promote his book *The Last Man on the Moon,* the museum administration announced there would be no autographs. Marj, however, found an opportunity to discreetly hand him a picture taken eighteen years earlier of her presenting him with the *kráslice* egg she had painted for him. Cernan studied the picture of the two of them, and then declared, "Oh! That looks like we were having fun." Smiling, he autographed the back of the picture. Marj cherishes that memento to this day.

Secretary of State Madeleine Albright

Our final story is about the pin presented to former Secretary of State Madeleine Albright. She was scheduled to be at the museum to open the traveling exhibition entitled *Read My Pins: The Madeleine Albright Collection.* The exhibition included two hundred and eighty dazzling pins. Some were inexpensive costume jewelry, others ultra-expensive designer pins with rare jewels.

All had been selected for their historical significance. To paraphrase the exhibition catalog, the Secretary of State wore pins to all of her negotiations: to emphasize her thoughts; to signify her hopes; to protest the absence of progress; or to show pride in the accomplishments of our country. There were also pins related to family and heritage.

The Madeleine Albright gift would come from The Guild of the museum. Determining exactly what the gift should be became a lengthy process, as the Guild is a truly democratic body. There were those in the organization who felt the gift should not be a pin, as she already had too many pins. Another segment felt just the opposite. Madeleine's own words settled the issue. In her book she said, "You might think that enough would be enough, but to an aspiring collector, every addition is exciting.... When presented with a gift-wrapped box, I ripped the ribbons off with heartfelt thanks and relish." Thus our gift would be a pin.

The next issue to resolve was exactly what kind of pin? It must have a message. What would the message be? Two months later after turning down designs by artists from the University of Iowa, Guild President Diane Hayes appointed a committee to come up with a recommendation.

Carolyn and Mel Holubar, John and Sandra Hudson, Pat Martin, Marj Nejdl, Alyssa Olson, and Catharine Otto came together to discuss the problem.

After two meetings the group had a plan. The pin would reflect the Czech heritage; thus it would have significance for both Madeleine, the Guild, and the museum. It would be cut from copper by committee member Catharine Otto. She was an experienced coppersmith who taught the skill in the Amana Colonies. The copper would then be painted by committee member Marj Nejdl. The exact appearance of the pin was to be determined by the two artists.

When the committee reported to the next Guild meeting, they anticipated there would be demands to see a rendering before the group gave their final approval. That was not the case. Upon hearing that Marj was one of the artists, the Guild voted unanimous approval. That is an indication of the credibility Marj has developed over her years of service to the museum. In short, the Guild moved at the speed of trust.

The artists' final design was a three-dimensional copper heart signifying the depth of Czech heritage. The copper heart was treated with a water based acrylic finish, so that the metal would not turn green. When Marj painted her Czech folk art design on the copper that acrylic finish would also help the paint to adhere. The copper component became the bottom portion of the pin.

For the top portion, the artists chose an embroidered ribbon like those frequently used to decorate Czech folk costumes. The ribbon was purchased from the Czech Republic. A small copper ring was used to connect the top and bottom parts of the pin. The picture herein shows two completed pins and their wooden presentation box, all painted by Marj.

Kaleidoscope

Our Marj embodies all of the best traits of immigrant families from Czechoslovakia, a respect for freedom of expression, a love of family, a diligent work ethic, and a humble and gracious personality. Czech folk art has been a prominent part of Marj's life. We, the members of The Guild Writers of the National Czech & Slovak Museum & Library, are honored that Marj considers this place her home.

Former Secretary of State Madeleine Albright wearing the pin

created by Marj Nejdl and Catharine Otto.

If you would like to enjoy more about Marj Nejdl's art, we suggest the book co-authored by Marj Nejdl and Pat Martin, *Decorative Czech Folk Art: The Artistry of Marjorie Nejdl*. Pat has also been a volunteer with the museum from the early days. She is the author of several books related to Czech culture and published by Penfield Books.

Carol Wohlleben
1937 - 2016

Some call her a risk-taker. Some call her an innovator. But many who knew her at Kirkwood, call her a pioneer. Carol was the visionary, the designer, the implementer, and the director of the Kirkwood Community College Hospitality Program. Beginning in 1972 with just twelve students, Carol has jumpstarted the careers of hundreds and hundreds of students for over twenty-five years. Today, the Culinary Arts Program at Kirkwood is recognized as one of the top twenty programs in the country.

There is no one who can tell the story but Carol. Read on to learn about her dedication to students, her indomitable spirit, her creative efforts, and her triumphs amid seemingly brick walls. There are still lessons to be learned from this life-long educator.

The Class Act

As my high school days were coming to an end, I began to focus on college. While in high school, the school counselor talked many girls into pursuing secretarial skills and nursing. She insisted studying typing and shorthand skills were what most of the female population would do. It was not common to argue with the counselors and teachers. We did what we were told. In the 1950s women had fewer career choices compared to the present time. I had studied one year each of algebra, chemistry, and biology, but no other science courses. I achieved high grades in all my studies, which was important.

Iowa State College—now Iowa State University—became my destination. After all, it was a family tradition. Once enrolled in college, I followed the course of study required by the College of Home Economics. Ironically, other than the basic requirements, the majority of the classes were in science, math, management, nutrition, and general studies, such as speech and English. I did use my high school shorthand skills for taking notes and always typed my papers.

Summarizing four years of study, I ended up majoring in institution management with a minor in chemistry. There were five graduates in this field of study.

Two job offers I considered seriously upon graduation were a hospital internship in nutrition in New York, and an opportunity as a food service director for Bishops Cafeteria with general headquarters in Cedar Rapids, Iowa. Bishops had several cafeterias in other cities and intended to expand into other states.

I chose the corporate headquarters of the Bishop Cafeteria Company. It offered me opportunities to travel, train other people, and standardize the menus and recipes used throughout all of their restaurants. I instructed in standard work techniques, recommended physical design and layout for some of their cafeterias, and worked with the administrative staff.

One of the company initiatives I enjoyed working on was the design of a new course of study in hospitality management at Iowa State College. That was a big step for the restaurant industry and for the college.

Moving forward many years I found myself a stay-at-home mom. With my kids in school all day, I had a little more time, and started getting interested in food-related projects again. Some of these involved working with the school systems and especially the school lunch personnel. These projects took place in the evenings when my husband, Eldon, could be at home with the kids.

Kirkwood Community College was just getting established and working on ways to expand its student body. The college recruited students who needed to complete GEDs, and offered vocational classes for those looking to build their knowledge and skills.

One day I read an intriguing article in the paper describing how Kirkwood was working with inmates in the Anamosa Reformatory to equip them with employable skills for working in commercial kitchens.

I called the Kirkwood administrative office, expressing interest in the program and shared my credentials and work experience. I asked if there was a culinary arts or hospitality course of study at the school.

He replied, "No, but would you like to start one?"

The year was 1969.

The Planning Phase

Beginning a new post-secondary educational program for a community college became a challenging experience for me. I began working with one of the college's program directors, Doris Poindexter, to establish the mission and goals of the program. Then we needed to determine how the program's goals and objectives would be developed, and what would be necessary to accomplish the goals.

The teaching involved physical skills, knowledge, experience, and related areas of study. Working with state educational standards was also part of the educational design. The curriculum had to be designed to meet the requirements of an associate degree. This meant it would focus on math, English, human relations, sanitation and safety, marketing, science, nutrition, management, and culinary arts courses. It was a lot to coordinate!

We needed to prepare a budget, recruit faculty, and acquire classroom and lab space. Also, we needed to prepare marketing materials, strategies for recruitment, and procedures for enrollment. There was the need for commercial food preparation equipment, and decisions had to be made about student kitchen tools, textbooks, and uniforms. These functions didn't occur in a step-by-step process. A lot of activities were mixed in a given day.

The general education courses would follow the college's format for classes, such as accounting and business management. The production courses had to be specifically designed for the kind of products identified in each food study area. Food production, bakery, and culinary arts offered basic and advanced classes. We also required service management and purchasing. Sanitation and safety had to meet state regulations. Each course had to be designed with its objectives and specific, measurable goals. Then the course had to be written to clearly define each factor.

As program director I would teach all the production and program-related classes. The general education courses would be taught by the faculty in the business department. It was proposed that the program would be under the umbrella of the vocational education department. I put my foot down at this! With knowledge and conviction, I asserted this program needed to be under the umbrella of the business department, as it was management related to food service, restaurants, and hotels. The administration accepted my position.

In the meantime, the paperwork for the program was submitted to the State Board of Education for approval, which it received!

Marketing, public relations, and the business departments came together and worked on the marketing of the program to enroll students for the new program. Admissions had a list of students who had inquired about programs. With all these departments working together, plus talking with several existing restaurants, enough students were interested, interviewed, and enrolled in the Hospitality Program.

Recruitment was crucial. Even a well-planned program doesn't work if there are no students enrolled. The first class had twelve students. Over the years the students were mostly high school graduates, second career seekers, or those pursuing advancement in their careers. There were also a few students just interested in learning to cook as a hobby, and some who were undecided about their career path—why not be a cook!

In later years, as the program gained greater recognition, we enrolled artists aspiring to work with foods, photographers, a doctor looking for a career change, a minister, and even students with handicaps such as blindness and autism.

Where would the classrooms and food preparation areas be located? Linn Hall was the only building on the Kirkwood campus at the time. There was really only one choice. The available room measured 20 ft x 20 ft, with a standard door and two large windows. It was located near the library and bookstore.

The First Year

When the first class started in 1972, the classroom was furnished with only two six-foot tables, fourteen chairs, and a chalkboard. Lectures began in the small classroom. Arrangements were finalized with Prairie High School to use their home economics room for our lab.

This arrangement was a disaster! The students grumbled as they had to carry groceries and other supplies to Prairie. The high school kitchen space was often messy, and our students had to clean up before we could begin our own classes. Equipment got moved around a lot, and couldn't always be found when needed.

I was really stressed and upset. In frustration, I made an appointment with the Kirkwood president, Dr. Selby Ballantyne, who was instrumental in creating Kirkwood Community College. A meeting was set up with the president, Doris Poindexter, and me. We had worked very hard to bring this program together. It was important we provide the training facilities and personnel to make it really work. In the meeting I reported how willing the students were to help us make the program what it was supposed to be—a commercial culinary and restaurant management program.

At the meeting, after a little discussion, I said, "No way!" on Prairie. "We must have a lab in Linn Hall."

Selby was great. He understood, but questioned where we would get equipment, how soon could we get it, and where would the money come from to purchase it.

The students pitched in and found a used refrigerator. An Amana upright freezer was given to the program, which really didn't work, so we made it our cupboard instead. One of the administrators had an electric range left from a home remodeling project. And a paint-splattered and dirty commercial three-compartment stainless steel sink was also donated. Just outside the room, a metal cabinet was installed for storage of supplies. The students stripped and cleaned the hall door.

Everyone helped clean. The college employees updated the wiring and plumbing for the equipment. It all worked.

All those hurdles were overcome, and the lab was established in Linn Hall. The students were so supportive of this effort. After all, it was about trying to provide the best we could for them and their futures. So, the Culinary Arts/Restaurant Management Program began—again.

I don't think the students realized how unusual it was for a community college to have a culinary arts program. I had done some research, of course, in working on the program, comparing what Kirkwood was offering and what other schools were providing. There were not many culinary schools at that time. Some of them may have been closeted in other college programs, or may have been non-degree programs, emphasizing vocational skills.

I was well aware of some schools such as the Culinary Institute of America in Hyde Park, New York, Johnson & Wales University in Providence, Rhode Island, and Kendall Culinary College in Chicago. These programs were specifically for culinary arts, baking, and management. Most food programs at colleges at that time were enclosed in other programs such as Home Economics.

I was the only instructor, later to be the professor and director of the program. I taught food preparation procedures, special techniques, and the science involved in the work. English, math, and accounting were taught through written assignments in the purchasing, human relations, nutrition, and sanitation courses. Many of these courses were developed into full semester classes taught by the appropriate faculty as time moved forward.

At this time, food handling, sanitation and safety were being highly promoted by the Iowa State Health Department. I was also required to become certified in this area. This was a course I taught for over thirty years, even certifying some local food inspectors.

I discovered so many things that first year. Some of the students had very few math skills, and struggled with writing and reading. These factors affected everything I had to teach.

First Kirkwood culinary class. Helen Martin second from left. Carol Wohlleben second from right.

The Second Year

By the next year, I began to realize several of the students in the classes had no interest whatsoever in food service. When I asked why they were in this program, they told me that when admissions had asked them for their course of study, they answered that they really didn't know. So admissions had enrolled them in the cooking classes, believing any student could probably handle those classes.

Again, I had several conversations with the administration and admissions office. I stressed to the staff in admissions the challenges of this career field. Students needed to know many skills: management, dealing with people, business, finance, health and food safety, sanitation, accounting, and much more. One of the biggest challenges was the ability to train and help people develop skills working not only with employees, but guests in their business, and working with other businesses in the area. "Just cooking? Oh my!!!"

As the year continued, I noticed each student was building skills. The students spent an enormous amount of time together, and it was a wonderful way to bond and develop strong relationships. We had all been through so much to get here.

The people in Linn Hall also enjoyed the program, as wonderful aromas often floated through the air, and through the library and bookstore. The employees got to enjoy many food samples!

By the end of the first academic year, I realized and shared with the administration that I was drowning from all the time, work, and preparation. There truly was a need for a second staff member. It was agreed to hire a new instructor.

The first person that came to mind was Helen Martin, an African-American single mother in her mid-twenties. She had been the first student to apply to the Kirkwood culinary program. At that time she was employed in the catering kitchen at the University of Iowa Memorial Union, and was interested in expanding her knowledge and skills. I found her to be very talented, intelligent, and skilled well beyond the program as it was originally designed. She was experienced in all areas of production, academia, human relations, and food artistry. There was a growing trend in making food presentations more artistic and enticing for the guests. Helen was well-liked by her fellow classmates. The position was advertised, and two other candidates, as well as Helen, were interviewed.

The interview team made the decision that Helen was the most-qualified candidate! Thus, she joined me, and we became a very strong leadership team for the growing program. She was also the first African-American on the faculty at Kirkwood. It was a wonderful career opportunity for her, as she learned and advanced in the industry.

Helen was responsible for production and food purchasing. I taught all the other courses and directed the program. Helen was full of wonderful ideas for the future. She was a great symbol of what the future of Culinary Arts/Restaurant Management staff would exemplify—teamwork. From these early years to the present, there is a strong bonding of the faculty, feeling comfortable with sharing ideas, and pointing out possible improvements, and no matter what, always supporting one another.

Purchasing food and supplies was a big task. There was not yet access to commercial sources, such as Sysco,

Hawkeye Foods, and other companies. Once the order for the program classes was put together, we had to go to the grocery stores, pick up the food and supplies, bring them back to school, carry them in, and put them away.

When it came to establishing costs for the recipes, the students had another math challenge, especially determining quantity costs. The foods prepared were in smaller quantities, as we didn't have a way to serve or sell them. The students ate the foods, and sometimes staff might stop by and "taste" what the students had made.

Several years later, as I was unloading groceries from my car in the college parking lot, President Selby said, "Carol, you scare me to death!" Astonished, I asked him why. I felt I was a nice person and hated to be in any bad situations.

His response was, "Because I never know what you will do next! I am just so thankful, though, for all you have done for this program and for Kirkwood."

A New Phase

Rapids Vending Company was contracted to run a cafeteria for the college. They were located next to our classroom. There was a small commons area for people to purchase their food, mostly fast food, sit out in the open area, and eat. This area was open for everyone to study or relax.

Within a few years, as the college grew, Iowa Hall was built. It housed classrooms, offices, conference areas, commercial kitchen, huge storage areas with walk-in refrigeration and freezer, and a large cafeteria. The cafeteria was leased to Rapids Vending Company who hired their own food-service personnel.

Knowing earlier that Rapids Vending Company was moving to Iowa Hall, I initiated many discussions proposing to move our educational program into the space they had occupied in Linn Hall.

Remember that our program was still housed in one room! Taking over the vacated space and making some modifications would enable the program to grow and be more realistic in quantities of food prepared, equipment usage, marketing, purchasing—all of the additional skills and knowledge required for this field of work. Of course it would require revamping the curriculum.

Once the decision was finalized to move the program, things began to happen quickly. It was wonderful with Helen on board, as she brought ideas and recommendations adding to the overall success.

The new space we inherited now included areas for food preparation, production, cleaning, and service. There was a commercial three-compartment sink, cupboards, a meat slicer, a food steamer, a commercial oven, a grill, a griddle, and a walk-in refrigerator opening into a small walk-in freezer. Rapids Vending had installed a table-height dishwashing station, with pre-rinse and garbage disposal, commercial dishwasher, and drying area.

On the service side of the kitchen was a reach-in refrigerator, beverage and coffee equipment, food display cases, an ice bin, a serving counter, and a cash register.

An open area on the other side of the service area provided access to the bookstore and library. This was a large space, and I requested reducing the size and enclosing it so that it actually looked like a dining room. After several discussion sessions, the administration approved. The walls went up. Again there were many meetings in which the students asked to be involved. This was to be their restaurant. They painted and wallpapered the room. About a dozen tables and chairs were added. We expanded the menu adding soups, salads, and sandwiches. Menus were planned and printed.

The Class Act restaurant in the early 1970s.

The original classroom was converted into a bakery for the program. The bakery produced rolls, breads, cakes, pies, and many other pastries and desserts.

A few months after the school year had begun, the students decided there needed to be a name for the new restaurant. Everyone agreed! We opened the anonymous naming contest to all Kirkwood students. The proposed names were reviewed by a committee of students, faculty, and one administrator. The final decision was The Class Act. It was their class; their act was the preparation and presentation of the food each day. We later learned that the person who had submitted the winning name was none other than one of our own culinary students. To this day the restaurant name remains the same, and I hope it always will.

Since this was now a full operational business, upgrades in the curriculum were needed, expanding it to include courses in accounting, bakery, dining service, and Garde Manger, which is the art of cold food preparation. The purpose was to give the students more opportunity to be creative while maintaining and supporting industry standards.

We revised the curriculum to make it transferable to Iowa State University, enabling our students to continue their education to achieve a four-year degree in hospitality. Our program now offered a two-year associate degree in addition to a one-year diploma.

We upgraded the requirements on uniforms for both the labs and dining room. We worked with several businesses in the industry to secure better small equipment for the students to purchase, such as knives, thermometers, and measuring utensils.

Competition Team: Carol Wohlleben on the left. Helen Martin center.

Under the direction of Helen Martin, students began to do more artistic work. They did *chaud frois*, which is working with a cold gelatin-coating, carvings, tube designing, chocolate work, artistic breads, and much more. The students prepared and served many special dinners and presentations for the administration and other special events at the college. It meant a lot of packing, moving, unpacking, serving, and packing up again. It was quite challenging. By now, the culinary program was becoming widely recognized. Students even entered culinary competitions held annually at the National Restaurant Association Convention in Chicago.

For me personally, the study of food—its history, its art, its science—has been a passion. It has given me the opportunity to connect with family, friends, colleagues, and businesses locally, nationally, and internationally. I have enjoyed a challenging, invigorating, and satisfying career.

Epilogue

Today, the hospitality program at Kirkwood Community College has three majors: Culinary Arts, Bakery, and Hospitality Management. There are one hundred fifty students enrolled, seven full-time faculty, and an office associate. The students are involved in the operation of a full-service restaurant and bar, bakery and catering operation, and a four-diamond hotel. The restaurant is still called The Class Act.

The Class Act restaurant 2018
The Hotel at Kirkwood Center

Guidelines for Memoir

You need not be world famous or fabulously rich to give a priceless gift of heritage to your descendants. You need only write down a few of the many stories you have heard or told at family gatherings. Imagine how your heart might sing if you had a short remembrance or two about everyday thoughts or events written by your great-grandparents. What a gem!

We encourage you to give memoir writing a try. Everyone has a story to tell. As you have discovered in reading *Kaleidoscope* there are various ways you might share your story. Experiment with different writing styles until you find one that suits you.

When writing memoir, chronology is not important. Write about what you remember. You can jump back and forth across the decades; one day writing about your childhood, the next about aging, and the next about a sporting activity. That is perfectly fine and to be expected. Just write about what interests you that day. Length is not important. Some stories are only a paragraph, others several pages long.

If you find you need motivation, you might consider joining a writers group. Our group meets fortnightly and we get much more from our meetings than motivation. We also enjoy an afternoon of entertainment, education, friendship, and trips down memory lane.

If you cannot find a writers group in your community, consider starting one. Below we provide guidelines to get you started.

Writing Group Guidelines

Your goal is to keep your writers group motivated and stimulated, meeting upon meeting, year after year. That requires a framework and guidelines. The key component to your success will be your devoted use of *time constraints*: eight minutes for an author reading, five minutes for group critique.

There are multiple benefits in putting time constraints upon each presenter. In addition to including more readers in each session, short readings also enable listeners to stay focused. Thus the writer will receive stronger and more detailed critiques. Boredom is also forestalled when there are more presenters, as it ensures diversity of content and writing style. If a listener doesn't connect with the story of one writer, they can easily wait-it-out, knowing a different reader is just minutes away.

Few in your group are likely to be professional writers; therefore daily obligations may interfere with productivity. On those occasions, your members will appreciate the eight-minute time constraint. In fact, they may find there are times when they will only manage to write a paragraph or two, and other times when they might write nothing. That is okay. Even in those situations, those members can always provide a valued critique for their fellow writers.

Time constraints do not mean your group will write only short stories. You will discover that one of the enjoyable aspects of your meetings will come from the anticipation of waiting for the next installment of a longer story. If your group has a writer who believes the impact of their story warrants a longer timeframe, remind them that few people read a book from cover to cover in one sitting. Their challenge is to write in a manner that draws the reader or listener back to their words. If their story is diminished by a fortnight's interruption, perhaps they need a rewrite.

Suggested Guidelines:

1. **Day, time, and place:**
   a. Our group holds fortnightly meetings on Thursday afternoons from 2-4 pm. That schedule is never altered. If a meeting falls on a holiday, we do not meet, but neither do we alter the fortnightly schedule.
   b. Beginning our sessions at two o'clock does not interfere with luncheon meetings. Ending at four o'clock helps to avoid rush hour.
   c. Your meeting place will depend upon the needs of your members. We meet in the conference room of the National Czech & Slovak Museum & Library. Thus, there are no problems with handicap accessibility. Indoor parking keeps us out of the weather, which is important in Iowa's winter ice and snow.
   d. On days when the conference room is not available, the museum provides space for us in either a classroom or the library.
   e. In addition to museums that might provide free meeting space for your group, you might consider libraries, educational institutions, fraternal organizations, city recreational buildings, condominium meeting rooms, or conference rooms of banks or other businesses. In most cases all you need do is ask.

2. **Group size:** We limit active membership to a maximum of fourteen people. If you're doing the math, you realize that equals a little more than three hours, and our meetings only run for two. Not to worry. It is likely everyone prepared to read will have an opportunity. That is because:
   a. Not everyone will attend every meeting. Some members will be traveling, others will have

conflicting appointments, or a cold they courteously decline to share.

b. In spite of good intentions, one or two attendees will not be prepared to read.

c. Of those who are prepared, there will be those who do not require eight minutes. Poets in particular seldom use their allotted time.

d. On those rare occasions when an author is prepared but time has run out, they go to the head of the list for the following meeting.

3. **Guests:** We welcome guests to come and observe.

a. *If* there is time *after* the active members have read, or if the guest's host cedes their reading time, a guest is invited to read and receive group critiques.

b. When a guest has read four times, the active members may propose and vote upon that guest for active membership.

c. If there is no vacancy at that time, a positive vote results in an associate membership. An associate member does not join the reading rotation. They read only if time permits. Upon a vacancy, an associate member automatically becomes an active member.

4. **Reading rotation:** We reward productivity and attendance. The order of rotation is:

a. Active members who are prepared to read.

b. Active members who are not prepared to read

c. Active members who are absent.

d. Associate members if time is available.

e. Guests if time is available.

f. The rotation list is updated after each meeting.

5. **Moderator and record keeper:** In our Guild Writers the same person does both. You could choose to separate the tasks.

a. The moderator chairs the meeting, gently encourages group expectations, operates the timer, and keeps the meeting on schedule.

b. The record keeper records who is prepared to read, and who has read.

    i. To establish a reading rotation for the initial meeting you might just go in one direction around the table. All subsequent meetings will follow #4 above.

    ii. Some record keepers also record the title of what was read.

6. **Meeting Format:**

a. The meeting opens with an educational component. A volunteer reads for five minutes from a published work. The craft of writing is the intended focus. The reading may be specific writing advice, or a reader may simply select an author whose writing style they admire.

b. Two or three minutes of discussion of the educational component.

c. The Chair then determines which members are prepared to read.

d. The Chair then calls upon readers in the rotation mentioned in #4.

    i. Readings should be only works that are currently being written or revised.

    ii. Eight-minute readings,

    iii. Five-minute critiques.

    iv. A timer with a soft beeper, and a gavel will be useful.

Preparing to Read

Choose to read only works that you are currently writing or revising.

In advance of the meeting, practice reading your selection aloud. Because most of us read faster than we talk, you may find you have a tendency to speak too rapidly when reading aloud. A reading is actually a form of public speaking. Therefore, it should be much slower than your regular reading speed. It is even slower than normal conversation. Speak slowly and with emphasis. Enunciate clearly. Sit up straight in order to project your voice to the back of the room. Look at your audience. These suggestions may sound simple, but they require practice. Over time, your presentation skills will improve.

Time your reading. If it is longer than eight minutes, select a good stopping place and mark it. If in the meeting you hear the beeper before you finish, you may read to the end of the paragraph, then stop. Mark your place so you will know where to begin next time.

Plan to print out your selection in fourteen-point type or larger, with a space and a half between lines. Provide wide margins for taking notes during your critique.

Successful Critiques

Receiving a critique:

Critique is an important part of the creative process. Be prepared to listen and take notes. This is not, we repeat, *not* a time to defend your writing. This is a time to absorb other people's impressions of your work.

Let your notes rest for a few days before reviewing them. Then, you may decide to accept some critiques and reject others. It is important to openly consider each and every idea, question, or suggestion. After reflection you'll be ready to tighten, expand, clarify, or in some cases, ruthlessly eliminate a word, phrase, sentence, or even a paragraph. If you rewrite in a timely manner, you are more likely to remember relevant details of the critique.

Offering a critique:

Critiques should be honest and respectful. Begin with what you consider to be the writer's strong points. Reinforce the things you particularly liked in the reading. Follow with requests for clarification: questions, areas of confusion, requests for more information, or greater detail. Then you may offer suggestions. The more specific your critique, the greater the learning opportunities for everyone in the group.

Keep your comments focused upon the writing, *NOT* your own personal experiences. If the reading triggers memories of your own, make a note to yourself, and then write *your* story to present at a future meeting.

If the author has to explain their writing, make side comments, or add information to their story, suggest those things need to go into their rewrite.

HAPPY WRITING

Image Credits

Index of Stories

Made in the USA
Lexington, KY
06 January 2019